DATE DUE

GAYLORD   #3522PI   Printed in USA

The smart cookies'

GUIDE TO

Couples and Money

Earn More, Argue Less,

Achieve the Life You Want Together

The **smart cookies** with Jennifer Barrett

VINTAGE CANADA

VINTAGE CANADA EDITION, 2010

Copyright © 2010 Smart Cookies Money Mentoring Inc.

Published in Canada by Vintage Canada, a division of Random House of Canada Limited, Toronto, in 2010. Originally published in hardcover in Canada by Random House Canada, a division of Random House of Canada Limited, in 2010. Distributed by Random House of Canada Limited.

Vintage Canada with colophon is a registered trademark.

www.randomhouse.ca

Library and Archives Canada Cataloguing in Publication

The Smart Cookies' guide to couples and money : earn more, argue less, achieve the life you want together / the Smart Cookies ; with Jennifer Barrett.

Includes bibliographical references and index.

ISBN 978-0-307-35799-1

1. Finance, Personal. 2. Couples—Finance, Personal. I. Barrett, Jennifer II. Smart Cookies (Money mentoring group)

HG179.S5225 2010a   332.0240086'55   C2010-900858-8

Printed and bound in the United States of America

2 4 6 8 9 7 5 3 1

This book is for all of the couples working towards
the abundant life they deserve.

May the ideas and messages within these pages
strengthen your commitment and focus
to turning your dreams into reality.

Acknowledgments

We would first like to thank our incredible partners for their love, support, and great senses of humour. Thank you also for allowing us to openly share our financial trouble spots and triumphs with our readers.

To our extraordinary families: Your unconditional love, guidance, and continued encouragement allow us to spread our wings even further.

To our friend and partner on this project, Jennifer Barrett, thank you for not only rising to the occasion but for doing it with such speed and focus. We appreciate your talents and style. Thank you also to Victor Ozols, Jennifer's patient and supportive husband.

We owe a special thank-you (and a big group hug) to our editor, Susan Traxel. You are bright, generous, incredibly patient, and a valued member of the Smart Cookie team.

A huge thanks also to the hardworking team at Random House Canada, including our publisher, Anne Collins; Cathy Paine; and Amanda Betts.

To our manager, Justin Sudds: Thank you for your constant guidance and enthusiasm. With you at the helm, we are in good hands. Thanks also to the team at S.L. Feldman & Associates. A special thanks to Jane Samis who always seems to have the answer and never misses a beat.

Thank you also to our literary agent, Richard Pine, for your continued guidance and time.

We are also so grateful to the couples who shared their stories in these pages. Your candid responses are sure to inspire others. We appreciate your time and honesty.

Contents

Introduction

Staying on top of your finances when you're single can be tough enough. But add another person to the mix and it can seem downright daunting. Since the first Smart Cookies' book came out, we've been approached time after time by people who are getting their own money situation under control but feel out of sync financially with their partners in life. Even if you've got your own finances in order, it is inevitable that some sort of money issue will come up when you're part of a couple—and not just because one of you may be in better shape financially, but because you probably each have very different perspectives on money and how to manage it.

Maybe you're trying to save more money but he's a big spender. Maybe she earns a lot more than you do, but you still want to feel like you're contributing and having a say in how you manage your money together. Or vice versa. Maybe you're just not sure about things like how to split the bills, whether to merge your accounts, or how much of what you should each be responsible for if you earn different incomes. Or you felt like you were doing just fine financially— that is, until he lost his job, or you lost yours, and now you can no longer afford to buy that condo you've had your eyes on. *Or* you've found that you're suddenly struggling to cover the bills or plan for your future, and you're fighting all the time over money.

Couples and money is a hot topic! We wrote this book to address all of the nagging money questions and thorny situations that come up when you're in a relationship—whether you're just starting to get serious or you're already married. We compiled all of the queries we've received about money and couples from across the country over the past year—there have been *tons*—and in the following chapters we do our best to answer them. As with our first book, we think there is a lot to learn from firsthand experiences of financial woes and success stories, so we also interviewed several couples at different stages in their relationships. You'll read some of their stories, as well as ours, in the pages ahead.

If you're having trouble even bringing up the subject of money with your spouse, or the person you're dating, don't be discouraged. You're not alone. It's tempting to avoid the topic, especially when you're in a new relationship. You probably don't need to see the studies (though they do exist) to know that money can be a source of frustration, conflict, and, yes, even breakups. You probably know that from personal experience. The five of us certainly do.

When we wrote our first book, *The Smart Cookies' Guide to Making More Dough,* two of us had recently ended long-term relationships in which we'd ceded almost total control of our finances to our partners, partly in an effort to avoid conflict (though in both cases it had the opposite effect). When the relationships ended, we were not only left in worse shape financially, but we lacked confidence and were at a loss as to how to manage our own money. We each learned a painful lesson: No matter who takes the lead in managing a couple's money, both parties need to participate in the process.

We all have not-so-fond memories of issues that arose with past boyfriends over money; whether it was because of different spending styles, different expectations about who was responsible for what (even when it came to getting the cheque at dinner!), or different approaches to the way we made and managed our money. Looking back, it seems like the common thread was a lack of communication: We either ignored the problem or kept our concerns to ourselves until emotions hit the boiling point. By then we were so upset, it was tough to talk about money without it turning into a fight.

What we've learned is that by *not* talking about it early on, we really made things worse. Couples don't usually break up because they argue about money, they break up because they *wait too long* to talk about it. They avoid the subject until they reach the point where the consequences from their differences overshadow everything else, and it feels like it's too late to change. That doesn't mean that you can't stay together if you don't share exactly the same perspectives on money, but you need to be able to find some common ground. That's one reason why it's so important to talk about money *before* you even move in with someone—and especially before you get married. You need to make sure that you're compatible not just physically and emotionally, but financially, as well. Too often, we act as if that piece will just fall right into place. If we get along well, we think, we'll have no problem merging our money and managing it together, right?

Wrong. The truth is you may have wildly different expectations about how much money you want to have and how you want to use it. Sure, you can still find a compromise that works for each of you, but that will only happen if you have an honest conversation about your financial expectations—about the life that you want to have together, how you're going to pay for it, and who's responsible for what—*before* you walk down the aisle or co-sign a lease on an apartment together.

And yet very few couples do. Most put off that conversation until they're forced to have it. Maybe not until one of you loses a job. Or until the lease on your apartment is up and you see it as an opportunity to buy a place together, but your partner has hardly anything saved up (and no idea that you'd hoped to buy a home this quickly). Or until you're married and you get pregnant and then you both suddenly have to figure out how you're going to cover all the additional day-to-day expenses of having a baby—especially child care. Maybe you also need to get a bigger place to accommodate a child. Not the ideal time to discover that you're not on the same page financially. By then it's too late. One of you will be resentful, the other one will feel guilty, confused, or even angry. And any discussion is likely to end in an epic argument.

Dealing with money *seems* so straightforward. After all, it's just numbers, right? So why does the subject evoke such a jumble of emotions and provoke so many heated misunderstandings? It's because there are so many different meanings and expectations associated with it. Money can represent power, control, freedom, love, success, validation, stress, anxiety—or a mix of all of the above (in varying degrees, depending on how much money you have). So it can be tough to discuss money without dredging up some of those underlying associations. If we're not honest about the kind of life we each want to create, realistic about how much it will cost, and comfortable with how much each of us is contributing, we're setting ourselves up for major conflict down the road.

Even before we get to that point, though, money plays a role in how we perceive the people we date. We often judge ourselves and each other—if unconsciously—by how much we make, how we spend our money, and how well we manage it. If we're deeply in debt, for example, we fear we may be judged as a failure. If we earn too little, we worry that we'll be perceived as a burden by our boyfriend or girlfriend, or that our career won't be valued as much. If we earn too much, we fear he or she may feel emasculated or intimidated, or resent us. If we're upfront about wanting to have a lot of money, we worry that we'll be seen as greedy or superficial (rather than ambitious, successful, or just realistic, given how much it costs to raise a family nowadays). Yet it's hard to pretend that money doesn't matter, especially if we're struggling to cover our bills and unable to afford the life that we want.

Each of us tends to view money a little bit differently, depending on the role it played in our lives growing up: whether it was plentiful or scarce; whether our family talked openly about it or, more likely, considered it a taboo topic; and how much we were taught about how to make and manage it. All of that affects the way we look at money, and the habits we fall into, as adults. And more often than not, the guys we're with have a different take on it than we do. That's not a problem, necessarily, as long as we agree on an approach that works for both people. But getting there can seem nearly impossible sometimes—a treacherous path full of obstacles and detours that can leave us angry and upset, and ready to ditch our companion and forge ahead on our own.

Before you do that, read this book. We want you to think of this as a road map to help you find that common ground as quickly and painlessly as possible, without encountering too many bumps along the way.

We've been there ourselves. And we know how tough it can be to try to tackle some of the financial issues that come up when you're part of a couple—especially when you're still trying to get your own finances in order. But we also know, both from personal experience and from speaking with dozens of couples, that with the right tools and the right approach *every* couple can get there. In fact, talking about money and making financial plans and decisions together can actually bring you closer together and strengthen your relationship. And it can certainly save you a lot of heartache and stress down the road.

We've targeted this book at women since, well, we're women ourselves. And the majority of the feedback from our first book came from women who are currently in a relationship, or hope to be in the near future. But there are exercises in here for both you and your significant other, so be sure to share this book with your partner, too. It's a great way to get the conversation started.

The best part, we've found, is that when you synchronize your financial goals and agree on the part you'll each play to reach them, you'll achieve them much faster than you could have on your own. As a team, you're not only building a stronger foundation for your relationship, and for your financial goals, but for your future together. And that's the greatest payoff of all.

Are you ready to take the first step? Turn the page, and we'll help you get started.

About Us

One Cookie at a Time

ANDREA BAXTER

Andrea, a marketing director and brand strategist, had no savings, a big mortgage, and $18,000 in consumer debt, including a revolving line of credit and two credit cards—one of which had gone into collections. Unfortunately, this was a result of one too many shopping sprees and non-fat lattes! Andrea had big dreams for herself, but figuring out how to get there financially was not her strong suit. Within a year of joining the Smart Cookies in early 2006, she'd paid off more than one-third of her debt. In 2007, Andrea paid off all of her debt and is now putting money towards building a savings account.

ANGELA SELF

Before becoming a Smart Cookie, Angela's motto was "spend now, worry later." She was living life to the fullest and relying on her high-interest credit card to foot the bill. She was clueless when it came to her finances and had no solid plan in place to make her big dreams a reality. After becoming a Smart Cookie, Angela switched career paths and also took on additional work to ensure she would be well on her way to financial freedom. She loves finding creative ideas to make money and build wealth without sacrificing social life or sanity.

KATIE DUNSWORTH

Katie, a newlywed and publicist, had a dark financial past full of maxed-out credit cards, shopping sprees, and unpaid bills. After meeting her husband and connecting with the other Smart Cookies, Katie committed to changing her ways. By taking a no-nonsense approach to career and wealth, she has made nearly $200,000 through investing in real estate and the stock market. Katie also managed to pay for her $22,000 wedding in cash while still continuing to build her savings and investment portfolio.

ROBYN GUNN

As a social worker, Robyn chose a career that she was passionate about but one that would not necessarily bring her riches. Also, she had accrued more than $12,000 in debt since divorcing two years earlier, and was struggling to keep up with bill payments on her limited income. After becoming a Smart Cookie, she has learned that she *can* have it all. She has found personal fulfillment and doubled her earning potential by obtaining her master's degree in social work. She is now debt free and has purchased her second condo, which she shares with her pampered pooch, Lucy.

SANDRA HANNAH

Sandra, a public relations manager, had $2,000 in credit card debt, a fear of managing money, and was quickly depleting her savings account trying to pay off her debt while supporting her active, single lifestyle. Today she has paid off her debt and put thousands into a retirement savings plan. With a newfound confidence, she is living the life she always imagined, as a young, savvy, independent city girl.

chapter 1

The Other "M" Word

Why Money Is So Hard to Talk About

Admit it. It's been on your mind since you realized you might be falling in love, even if you wouldn't dare say it out loud: Is he (or she) in good financial shape? Will we be able to build a future together? Forget about marriage, money is the *real* "M" word.

No matter how often we tell ourselves that money doesn't matter when we're in love, we know it does. Love can bring us joy and companionship. But as the Motown song made famous by the Beatles goes, "Your loving gives me such a thrill, but your loving don't pay my bill[s]!" To actually build a life together as a couple, you need more than love. You need a financial plan.

But here's the good news: Being in a long-term relationship can be as good for your wallet as it is for your heart. With a plan in place, you have the potential to achieve your financial goals a lot sooner as a couple than you could on your own.

Pool your savings, for example, and you can buy a home much sooner than with only one income—not to mention a bigger one. Together, you may also be able to qualify for lower mortgage rates or interest rates on a car or bank loan, saving you thousands of dollars in interest. And by combining your savings into one account, you are more likely to meet the high minimum balance required to qualify for some of the best-yielding money market accounts.

You can cut costs in other ways, too. How about a date night *in?* Cook something yummy for dinner or share some cheap takeout and snuggle on the couch with a movie—it can be just as enjoyable as an evening out, and a lot less expensive! All of this translates into more money for both of you. If you and your partner already live together, you know that you can also dramatically cut your expenses by splitting the rent or mortgage and the bills, and maybe even by selling one of your cars and sharing the other. Katie and her husband, Nick, have done both, and saved thousands of dollars in the process.

Being part of a couple can also mean you've got another source of financial support if you need some short-term help, and someone who won't charge you interest on a loan. (At least, we hope not!) And over time, your incomes are likely to fluctuate and there will be periods when one of you has to lean on the other. Being able to do that can actually help you reach your goals even faster than you could on your own. Robyn helped her former husband out financially when he went back to school, and then he returned the favour when she started a graduate degree program and cut down her shifts at work. With his help, she was able to take additional classes and get her degree much sooner than she would have otherwise. That also meant that she was able to increase her income faster, now that she qualified for higher-paying jobs with the additional degree.

When Angela and a former boyfriend moved in together and decided to combine their finances, he had double the debt that she did from school. Nonetheless, they consolidated their balances and worked together to pay the debt off faster. Then, when she graduated and took a freelance position that offered her the chance to hone her skills but without a steady paycheque, he helped support her financially between projects so she could get the experience she needed to land a more stable, better-paying job.

There are less tangible advantages to being in a committed relationship, too: It often forces you to take a hard look at your own financial habits. When you know that your actions affect your partner, too, you're more likely to pay attention to what you're doing with your money. And you've got extra motivation to set aside money for future goals if you know your partner is doing the same.

When Sandra and her boyfriend, Jason, began dating, they often surprised each other with gifts and extravagant dates: tickets to a hockey playoff game or a concert, or a day of spa treatments. For a while, Sandra didn't worry about how much they were spending on each other, since she enjoyed spoiling her boyfriend and he was happy to return the favour. Plus, they were both making good money, and neither was depending on a credit card. But as they became more serious, Sandra began to worry that they wouldn't be able to keep up those kinds of splurges without dipping into their savings. By this point, they'd talked about their future together and she knew that if they spent too much now, they would pay for it later. So when they started talking about taking a trip to Hawaii, she saw it as an opportunity for both of them to rein in their spending a little. Sandra calculated how much it would cost and then they discussed how much they'd each have to set aside if they wanted to take the trip within the next six months. Once they had a tangible goal and put it in perspective, they knew that in order to save enough money they'd have to start eating in more often, plan less expensive outings together, and skip some of their habitual Starbucks runs. But each of them thought it was worth the trade-off. All it took was a little incentive, and in the end it helped both of them get into the habit of saving money each month for their future goals.

These kinds of behavioural changes that happen when you're in a serious relationship may help to explain why those who are married tend to increase their personal wealth at a much faster rate than those who are single. One 15-year study by Ohio State University (published in the *Journal of Sociology* in 2005) found that those who stay married are able to accumulate nearly *double* the wealth of those who remain single. The study's author, research scientist Jay Zagorsky, attributed the difference to the benefits couples get by splitting expenses and combining their savings, as well as the new attitude many of them develop about money. He noted that the realization among married participants that their actions now had consequences for at least one other person—and maybe children, too—prompted many to adopt better financial habits and put more money away rather than spend it.

The U.S. census, which also tracks wealth, seems to support these findings. They found that the average net worth of all households headed by married couples is nearly $102,000, while single men have an average net worth of $23,700 and single women have an average net worth of just $20,217. In this case, if you split the total net worth in half for married couples, each spouse has a net worth that's *more than double* that of their single counterparts. That's a big difference.

The Canadian census tracks earnings, not net worth. But it found that childless couples have an average combined income of $59,834, while couples with kids earn nearly $83,000 combined. Meanwhile, the average income for singles living on their own is just $24,808. Even if you divide the income in half for couples with at least one kid at home, that means each partner is still making nearly 68 percent more on average than their single counterparts. True, age may be a factor here: More singles are in their 20s or 30s, so their earnings won't be as high as those who are more established in their careers—but that's not enough to account for the whole difference. It's likely that being in a committed relationship, especially if you have a family to support, can also provide a powerful impetus to work harder, or to seek a better-paying job or additional sources of income.

Of course, if you want to enjoy all the financial advantages of being part of a couple, you need to keep an open line of communication about money and always work together to plan your financial future. Once you know exactly how much you need to earn or save to reach your goals, you'll be more motivated to earn enough to stay on track—especially if you know your partner is doing his or her part. (We'll give you some ideas on easy ways to earn extra income in Chapter Six.) Which is one of the reasons why we don't just want to help you identify your goals, but encourage you to put a price tag on them as soon as possible so you know exactly what you need to achieve them.

Working through your finances as a couple and planning your future together won't just improve your finances: It can actually improve your relationship, too. Working together to achieve the things that you both want can be a fun process, once you're both on the same page. Katie and her husband say they've actually come to look forward to their monthly "money dates," a time they set aside to talk about investment ideas, monitor the progress they've made towards their financial goals, celebrate their successes, and help each other tackle any challenges that have come up. Talking about money has become so habitual that the once-taboo topic often drifts into their daily discussions too, whether they're sharing news on a deal they got that day or discussing the pros and cons of an investing tip or strategy they read about in the financial news.

Still, that doesn't mean that bringing up the topic the *first* time is easy. Even Katie admits that getting to that level of comfort took a lot of practice and there were some uncomfortable, even emotional, conversations over money in the beginning of their relationship. Maybe that's why so many of us try to avoid the topic for so long. Sure, we'll talk with each other about the things we want in life. But we often put off discussing the one thing we *need* in order to have them: money. We manage to talk about how we'll split the bills for the wedding or the utilities and rent, but dance around the bigger questions of how we'll merge our money or save enough for the life we each envision. Too often, we just assume that piece will fall right into place on its own: As challenges come up, we figure, we'll deal with them then. If we get along well, we should have no problem sorting out the financial stuff down the road, right?

Maybe not. Beneath the surface, you could each have wildly different expectations about how much money you need to live the life you want—and you're not likely to know unless you talk about it. Yes, you can still find a compromise that works for both of you. But to do so, you need to know how each of you envisions your life together, how you'll pay for it, and who's responsible for what. Ideally, you should have that discussion well before you walk down the aisle or co-sign a lease on an apartment together. But if you haven't, you're certainly not alone.

Money Talks

A poll conducted for the Bank of Montreal in 2008 ranked money as *the* most sensitive topic of conversation among Canadians—ahead of religion, politics, and even weight. So it shouldn't be a surprise that in the U.K., the Financial Services Authority found nearly three-quarters of couples have a tough time talking about money: One-third of the nearly 1,500 people it surveyed said they'd rather discuss sex or a previous relationship with their boyfriend or partner.

The bottom line is if you don't talk about your financial concerns and expectations with your partner there is a good chance that any assumptions you have made could turn out to be wrong. You might believe that the man you're with is financially successful because he has a hip wardrobe and almost always picks up the tab when you go out, for example, or simply because he works in a high-paying industry (even though you may have no idea what he's actually earning). You might think that since he rarely uses a credit card around you, he's got little or no debt. And when he talks about wanting to start a family, you're sure that means he's got money saved up. Unless there are obvious signs indicating otherwise—maybe you overhear a call from a collection agency or you're there when the landlord shows up to demand overdue rent—it's easy to assume that your boyfriend, or partner, will be able to contribute at least as much as you are financially to the relationship, if not more, right?

So you put off the money conversation until you're absolutely forced to have it. Maybe one of you loses a job and the other is stuck covering the bills because you don't have savings. Maybe you decide to buy a home together, only to discover that your partner's credit score is so low that you can't get a mortgage. Or you get pregnant and all of a sudden have to figure out how you're going to cover all the additional day-to-day expenses of having a baby— not to mention, child care or the bigger place you might need to accommodate a child. Of course, this is *not* the best time to realize that you and your partner are not on the same page financially. By then it could be too late, and you may find that both your finances and your relationship are in serious trouble.

We know this from experience. Each of the five of us can recall a relation-ship in which we put off talking about our finances and made assumptions that turned out to be wrong—and regretted doing so. From varying expecta-tions about who was responsible for what, to different approaches regarding making and managing money to coping with opposing financial priorities, we know how bad it can get. Had we discussed these issues with our partners sooner, we might have been able to reach a compromise we were both happy with. But the longer we waited, the harder it was to bridge the disparity in our habits and attitudes.

It may seem hard to believe that couples who are close in every other regard can be so vastly different when it comes to money, but researchers say it's more common than you might think—even among married couples. One study published in the *Journal of Socio-Economics* found that spouses disagreed on everything from how much income and wealth they had to how much debt they carried. "Most husbands and wives do not share similar views of the family's finances," the research scientist concluded. Even worse, they often didn't realize it, which means they might assume their finances are in better shape than they actually are and behave accordingly. That's not good for their relationship or their finances.

When it comes to what's important to each person financially, couples don't score much better. In a 2006 *Money* magazine survey of 1,000 spouses, about a quarter of the men surveyed said they thought their wives believed that having the right investments was very important. The actual number was nearly *twice* that. Likewise, only 45 percent of men said that having cash stashed for emergencies was very important to their wives but, in fact, more than two-thirds of the wives said it was crucial. Meanwhile, women believed their husbands cared more about paying off debt and saving for big pur-chases than men actually said they did. Husbands and wives, the survey con-cluded, "just aren't getting through to each other about financial goals, priorities and worries." No kidding.

Having more money doesn't necessarily result in more conversations about it either. While 70 percent of wealthy wives said they shared the financial decision-making responsibilities with their spouses in a 2005 survey by PNC Advisors, fewer than half of their husbands said that was the case. (Most men said they were in charge, which was news to many of their wives.) The researchers found "an alarming lack of communication about wealth planning and goals, and significant differences between the sexes on financial topics—from control over finances to attitudes toward wealth—that can lead to greater problems down the road if not addressed."

And that's married couples! Those who are in a relationship, even if it's a serious one, are even less likely to broach the topic.

As we mentioned earlier, having *different* views on money—or inaccurate assumptions about your partner's views—doesn't mean you can't succeed as a couple. It just means that it's even more important that you talk about them. Katie and Nick, for example, realized early on that they didn't always agree on how they spent their money, or even how they managed and invested it. But they were able to overcome their differences by getting them out in the open and coming up with a plan that worked for both of them. (We'll explain how they did that in more detail in the coming chapters.)

All five of us have learned that it's usually not the differences themselves that threaten the relationship, but the unwillingness to discuss them. By not talking about money early on, we really make things worse. Couples don't break up because they argued about money. They usually break up because they wait until they're in a bind to bring up the topic, and then it's often too late. By that point, if they realize that they have very different values or views when it comes to money, they may not be willing or able to reconcile them. That was the case with two of us in past relationships that ended.

Talking about money and finances can also reveal a lot about your overall goals and values. And if you discover when you have that conversation—as some of us did—that you and your partner have opposing goals or principles, then money isn't the only issue. If you don't share the same core values in a relationship and you're not working towards the same things, it's very hard, if not impossible, to build a successful future together no matter how much money you have. That's another reason why it's so important to talk about money *before* you move in with, or marry, someone. You want to make sure that you're compatible not just physically and emotionally, but financially. (Check out our money type guide in Chapter Four to see how you match up as a couple.)

So why is it so difficult to have that first conversation? See if any of these sound familiar to you:

We've been told most of our lives that it's impolite to talk about money.

Few of us are accustomed to talking about our finances *at all*—even with our closest friends or family. So why should it be any different with the people we date? Before we formed our money club in 2006, none of us were really comfortable talking about money with anyone. The prospect of spilling the intimate details of our finances with four other women, even in a completely confidential setting, was more than a little nerve-racking. Now of course, we're glad we did. Both our finances and our friendships have improved because of it. Still, we know that bringing the subject up with the person you're involved with can be tricky, especially in the beginning of your relationship.

You may be wondering how much he earns, how much debt he has, and whether he can support himself and maybe a family, too. But you're not likely to ask him right away. Asking him about his financial status can seem as intrusive as asking for details of his past relationships, or looking through his email. And, even if your own finances are in pretty good shape, you may be reluctant to talk about your own income, how much you spend on clothes or nights out with your friends, or how much debt you might be carrying. You may worry that, if you're doing well, sharing the details of your financial status could be misinterpreted as bragging. And if you're not in great financial shape, you may fear that he'll judge you harshly for mismanaging your money, or be turned off by the thought of having to shoulder your financial burden.

Robyn, who's now in a long-term committed relationship, remembers being reluctant to ask too many questions about past boyfriends' finances because she never wanted them to think that she was after their money or with them for financial reasons—even though she was perfectly able to take care of herself and they could likely see that. She felt particularly uncomfortable prying for details, especially if the man she was with seemed reluctant, or defensive, about providing them. So she'd often just drop the subject. (Note to readers: There's usually a reason why he's acting that way, and it may come back to haunt you later if you don't persist.)

In North America, we've been brought up to believe that money is an extremely private matter. Few of us know how much our closest friends earn or how much debt they have. So it may seem rude to pose those questions to our partner. But here's the difference. You can argue that knowing how much your friend earns, or how much she owes, isn't any of your business because it has no real effect on you—unless she's been crashing at your place rent free, or you've loaned her some money. But your partner's financial status *is* your business if you plan on sharing your lives and having a future together because it has a direct effect on you. If you move in together and he can't pay his half of the rent, you're stuck with it. If he has a terrible credit score, it will affect both of you when you try to get a mortgage or a car loan. If he has a lot of debt he hasn't told you about, that may mean you both have to postpone plans to get married, buy a home, start a family, or even take a vacation. If he earns less than you, you may be responsible for covering more of the bills. And vice versa. You're no longer in it alone. You're in it together. So, once you are in a committed relationship, you both have every right to know each other's financial details. That doesn't mean divulging them won't be difficult, though, especially if either of you are in financial trouble since . . .

It's embarrassing to admit that our own finances aren't in great shape.

Even though the five of us were committed to improving our finances and to supporting one another, it was still tough for Sandra to admit (at our first Smart Cookies meeting in 2006) that she'd blown right through the $8,000 she'd so diligently saved while living at home—and now had credit card debt, too. Angela and Robyn were equally sheepish as they explained to the group how they'd pretty much given up control of their finances to their exes in relationships that had recently ended, so they had little confidence or experience managing their own finances, which were in total disarray at the time. Even Katie, who made the highest salary among us, winced as she revealed that she had become such a shopaholic that she actually hid new purchases from her then fiancé. And Andrea remembers being petrified to admit to the rest of us that she owed $18,000 on her credit cards. She was worried that the people she liked and respected—including her boyfriend—would think she was a failure, or a fraud, if they found out how much debt she'd accumulated trying to maintain a lifestyle and wardrobe she couldn't afford.

Before she joined the Smart Cookies, Andrea remembers being reluctant to reveal any details about her debt to her then boyfriend, even though they were living together. She knew he assumed that she was good with her money because she conveyed an image of success: a high-powered career in marketing, designer clothes, and a chic *Sex and the City* lifestyle. He had no idea how much of it was really being financed through her credit cards. "When we finally started talking about money, he found out that I was bad at managing it—actually, that I wasn't really managing it at all!" she remembers. "He was shocked." She'd considered her debt and the way she spent her money to be such a personal matter that she was unwilling to talk about it, even after they moved in together and started splitting expenses. At first, it was easy to pretend that she had everything under control—especially since he had no idea that it actually wasn't. By the time she admitted her financial shortcomings, overspending was no longer the only issue. It became a matter of trust and honesty. He wondered why she hadn't been upfront with him earlier, and worried about whether there were other issues she was holding back. Andrea felt guilty about not opening up to him sooner and putting them in a worse financial situation because of it. The awkward feelings that followed weren't the only reasons why they eventually broke up, but they were certainly a contributing factor.

Of course, Andrea was so worried about admitting to her own financial faults that she didn't stop to think that even if her boyfriend was good with money then, that may not have always been the case. Chances are, you're not the only one who's made mistakes with your money. In fact, sharing your money woes might actually make your partner more comfortable opening up about his or her missteps with money, too, and bring you closer. We found that to be the case when we formed our money group. It was a little nerve-racking for each of us to confess the details of our financial situations at that first meeting of the Smart Cookies: how much we made, how much we owed, and how much we needed to learn about managing our money. But it was also a great relief. Admitting our own money mistakes, and learning about the financial faux pas that our friends had made along the way, actually made us feel less anxious about our situations and created an immediate bond between us.

Even if your significant other is one of those rare types who has always been responsible with money, a relationship means that *you're in it together now*. It's in both of your best interests to work as a team towards turning your finances around. And don't beat yourself up if he's better with money than you are! Remember that being able to manage your money successfully is just one skill that you can bring to a relationship. There are surely other areas in which you have more experience or expertise and he can learn from you. When you're dealing with money matters, as with any challenge in a relationship, you both need to be honest and supportive with each other—willing to listen, without judging, and to help. Even if he's got a great record when it comes to managing money, he might still learn from some of your mistakes. Though, of course, that means you must first be willing to admit them.

Talking about it will force us to confront our financial reality.

Being embarrassed about admitting that your finances are in shambles is one thing. But another big reason none of us had wanted to address our money problems until the first Smart Cookies meeting was because it would force us to acknowledge that we weren't happy with the way things were working out financially, and that it was time to take responsibility for the mistakes we'd made, or were still making. And we knew that would probably require some big changes in the way we spent and managed our money.

Those same concerns often keep us from talking about our finances with the people who are closest to us. In fact, it can be even harder to talk about it with our partners. As we said earlier: Friends have each other's best interests at heart but, usually, no real personal stake in each other's finances. But that's not the case when you're seriously involved with someone. The financial decisions you make will have lasting consequences for both of you. And that can be a scary thing to think about—especially when you don't feel like you've been making the best decisions yourself.

KATIE'S STORY

One thing I knew for sure was that starting the conversation about money wasn't going to be comfortable. I didn't think there'd be a blow-out screaming match, but I knew it would mean change. And even after my husband and I first got engaged, I still looked at my spending habits as my own business, as long as I was using my own money. It didn't hit me that my decisions were now affecting both of us. After we announced our engagement, I realized I was regularly spending $200 to $300 at a time on things like clothes, hair products, and jewellery, all in the name of "the wedding and honeymoon." As my pile of purchases slowly took over our dining room, my fiancé, Nick, suggested we make a budget. At first, I bristled at the thought: Why should I be held accountable for how I spent my own hard-earned money? The nerve! I should be able to do whatever I want with it, right? For months, I angrily dodged any money-related conversations. None of your business, buddy, I would think to myself.

The situation finally hit home when Nick presented me with a well-researched plan to rent out the second bedroom of our tiny apartment to an international student. I flew off the handle. Why on earth would we do that? With sadness in his eyes, he calmly explained how he felt that in order to move towards achieving our common goals—starting a family, buying a home, and having the freedom to travel where and when we wanted—we needed more money. I argued that we both made good salaries and we didn't pay that much in fixed expenses, and for a minute he didn't say anything. And that's when it hit me: As Nick was relentlessly planning and saving for our future, I was frittering away my income on myself. I was buying things that might give me a temporary lift but were keeping me from saving for the things I really wanted to get out of our life together. That was a huge breakthrough moment for me. I came clean, and I agreed to—finally—have that dreaded money conversation and put together a budget. And I vowed from then on to work on our finances together. So we decided to set aside one day each month to review our financial goals and to look at investment opportunities. Now that we both feel comfortable talking about it, discussing spending and saving is a part of our daily conversations, so we're always clear on where our money is going. I'm so glad we did. Cutting back on my spending wasn't easy at first, but it's one of the reasons why we were able to pay for our dream wedding—in cash—and to afford a great condo downtown. And, I realized, I never really missed not having another pair of jeans or more jewellery—especially when it meant being able to have the things I truly wanted and to know I was helping us move closer to the goals we'd created together.

Of course, you may not be the only one with financial problems to fix before you can build a future together. You might find out that he's a lot worse with his money than you are.

You fear his finances may be in worse shape than you thought (or hoped).

A friend of ours was in a relationship with a man who spoiled her endlessly. At first we were all a bit envious. He took her to Paris, bought her expensive clothes, and wined and dined her at all the top-rated (and priciest) restaurants in the city. She assumed that he could afford such a decadent lifestyle and must be doing really well financially. It wasn't until *after* they got married that she discovered the ugly truth: That he had been charging almost everything on his credit cards. And he'd racked up an enormous debt. She might not have enjoyed her cashmere sweater, or that five-course dinner, as much had she known that she'd eventually be paying for it herself—plus interest!—once they were married. Sure, everyone loves to be pampered, but if you plan on staying together, you better make sure you know where that money is coming from—and whether it's worth borrowing against your future to impress you now.

Sandra put off bringing up money with her boyfriend, Jason, for months, even though she was worried that they were spending too much on each other. Things were going so well that she didn't want to cut their "honeymoon stage" short by bringing up heavy subjects like paying off debt and planning for a future together. Plus, she knew it would be challenging to figure out how to align their financial habits and make sure they were both putting money away for their future, not spending against it—especially when he'd become accustomed to using his money as he wished without having to be accountable to anyone. When it finally came up, they were able to talk about what they wanted and expected the other to contribute to their relationship financially. And planning the trip together to Hawaii helped, too, since it gave them a shared goal to which they could both contribute. It also gave her boyfriend a tangible reason to rein in his spending habits. She also encouraged him to spend less on her. Instead of eating out on their dates, one of them would cook a romantic dinner for the other. Instead of taking her to Starbucks for coffee drinks, they went downstairs to the complimentary coffee bar in his apartment building. Instead of spending a lot on afternoon activities, they'd hang out for free at the pool at his building. They had just as much fun together, but spent a lot less.

The reality is committing yourselves to working together on a financial plan and to contributing equally (or, as close as you can, depending on the incomes you earn) is akin to committing yourselves to each other. It's a big step in a relationship, and a crucial one. If either of you continues to spend—or to use a credit card—as if you're still single, you're just pushing your future together further away and risking the chance that one of you will end up resenting or distrusting the other for it.

The Importance of Being Honest

It's not surprising that many of us—especially if we're financially successful— worry about the consequences of falling in love with someone who isn't. What if you learn that he owes $20,000 on his credit cards? Or that he makes half of what you do? What if you discover that the reason he has that nice apartment is because his parents have been paying the rent? Or if he admits that they've never saved a penny or opened a retirement account?

You may be in love—or so you think—but how can you possibly start planning a future together? Having a frank discussion about your finances, and about your concerns, is the first step towards doing that. If you're both willing to work on your bad habits, and committed to contributing your fair share to reach your financial goals, then you can make them happen (albeit, maybe a little slower than you'd hoped). But if they're not willing to change, or even to talk about their financial faults, the reality is that you may not have a future together—well, unless you're willing to foot the bill for it. And that's a lot to ask of someone.

Give him some time, though, especially after you first bring up the subject. You're a team now. That means he shouldn't have to do this all on his own. You can help by being supportive emotionally and maybe even helping to pay down your partner's debt (think of your future!), or picking up some of the bills while they do.

Katie admits it took her a little while to fess up to her then fiancé that she was overspending on things for herself—at the expense of goals they had together—and to improve her habits so that she was contributing to their future, too. She found that it's just as tough, if not tougher, for a man to concede his mistakes—especially if he was overspending on you! Men often feel additional pressure because of their traditional role as providers. (Many of their fathers may have been the *sole* breadwinners, after all, supporting an entire family.) So it's really difficult for some to admit that they're not even doing a good job of providing for themselves, especially if they've led you to believe otherwise.

If you want to stay together, though, it's essential that you talk about it. Both of you need to feel as if you're each contributing to the relationship, no matter how much you're earning or owe. And he needs to behave financially as if he's part of a couple now, not a bachelor trying to woo a woman with expensive gifts and dinners. As we said earlier, once you're in a committed relationship, the financial decisions you make can affect both of you—even if you're using your own money.

The good news? We know from personal experience and from talking with dozens of couples that if you can agree on your goals, and you are each willing to take steps to improve your finances and to play your part in reaching those goals, then you can have a wonderful future together *even* if you're a financial mess right now. (We'll help you each get your finances in order in the coming chapters, too.)

You're worried you'll discover you have very different financial priorities or goals.

If you've based your vision of the future together on assumptions you've made and not *actual* conversations, you may not want to know otherwise—even if you suspect it. After all, what if you discover that you either have different goals or very different ideas about how you're going to reach them? That may leave you questioning your future together altogether. So, instead of talking about it, you simply clam up, avoid the conversation, and hope for the best (e.g., that he'll change his mind, or come to his senses, without you nudging him).

We probably don't need to tell you that this isn't the best approach. If you don't discuss your goals and views on money, you may end up learning about them the hard way or allowing the gap between your goals to grow wider and wider. That makes it harder to find a compromise down the road, as Angela found out.

ANGELA'S STORY

My former boyfriend and I picked up David Bach's book, *Smart Couples Finish Rich*, when we moved into our first place together. We were actually excited to read it and get started on working together to improve our finances. At least we thought we were. The first exercise we did required us to each list our most important values and then create common goals based on those values. He picked power, freedom, and independence. My choices were completely different: happiness, family and friends, and making a difference. I wasn't too worried about it initially. But then we mapped out our financial goals based on these values. As we read them off, we discovered that we had completely contrasting ideas of our future together. We took one look at each other's goals, tucked our papers into the book, and left the topic alone. It was clear that we had very different intentions about what to do with our money and at that time, neither of us was willing to change our goals or the spending and saving habits that we'd adapted. We thought that if we just stopped talking about it, we could avoid any problems. But we quickly learned that the real problem wasn't our different views on how to manage our money; it was the fact that we weren't willing or able to talk about it as a couple, to resolve our differences and come to some sort of compromise we both could live with. We ended up breaking off the relationship a few months later, in part because we'd convinced ourselves that we had incompatible ideas about our futures, even though we'd never given ourselves a chance to resolve them.

So, what happens if you and your partner find out that you don't have the same goals? In some cases, you may determine that they're not so far apart. If one of you wants to start a family a little sooner than the other, for example, you may be able to adjust your expectations a little to find a compromise. What if one of you wants to live in the city, while the other one wants to move to the suburbs? Why not try to find somewhere in between that captures some of the qualities that you like about each (a suburb with a main street, for example, where you can live above storefronts or near a train station)? Maybe having a big cushion of savings is really important to one of you, but the other one likes to be able spend a little more regularly on travel, home repairs, or new furniture. Why not come up with a figure that you're both okay with leaving in the account—we recommend an amount that would cover about three to six months' worth of bills and expenses—then agree to use any additional savings towards vacations or other purchases? Or, set up another savings account and start a separate vacation or furniture fund. By talking about your differences, you can often find a way to bridge them and come up with a plan that works for both of you, even if it's not exactly the same as the one you had in mind initially.

Having slightly differing visions for your future together, or different priorities when it comes to how you spend your money, really isn't unusual. The trick is coming up with a plan that takes each of your visions and priorities into account. That could mean putting some of your personal goals on hold, temporarily, or reassessing what's really important to you. But, as we've found, the result can be even better than the life you'd imagined (in part, because you're sharing it with the person you love). We'll show you how to do that in Chapter Three.

Of course, there's always the chance that your goals are completely incompatible. Maybe you want to take at least one big vacation each year, while he hates to travel and prefers to stay home and spend any extra money renovating the house that you think is perfectly adequate as it is. Maybe buying a home is really important to you, but he prefers to rent and spend any extra savings on weekend trips and dinners out with you and his friends. Often, money isn't really the issue in these cases, it's lifestyle. But how you want to spend it reveals a lot about your underlying values and goals. If yours are very different from his, then you have to come up with a reasonable compromise, or acknowledge that your relationship just might not be the right fit.

Getting the Conversation Started

Don't worry. You don't need to do it on the first date, or even the tenth. What you each do with your money won't become a big issue until it's clear that you are committed to a future together. But as soon as you're in a serious relationship and are talking about sharing your future, it's time to talk about money, too.

So, how do you bring it up?

Well, you can always use this book as an excuse. But there are other ways to broach the topic, too. Maybe you've got something you're saving for together, whether it's your wedding or just a romantic vacation. As you make your plans, you can use it as an opportunity to talk about some of your other goals and even create a spending plan together, like Sandra and her boyfriend did when they planned their trip to Hawaii (see Chapter Six). If you have some money saved up, you could suggest that you move that into a joint high-interest savings account and that you both put a set amount into the account each month so that you'll have the money for something you both want—or just to keep as an emergency fund for unexpected expenses.

Or, if you're talking about moving in together, expand the conversation about how to split bills and expenses to include talking about setting money aside for your future goals too. That is a great way to start figuring out how you can work together to manage your money and achieve your goals.

Or try the reverse. Ask him if you can spend some time tonight or this weekend talking about your plans for the future. Trying to figure out how you can reach those goals together is a natural way to ease into a more detailed discussion on money. And it will help keep you focused on building a future together, rather than dwelling on any differences you may have in your finances now. You can use the Perfect Day exercise in Chapter Three to help you come up with a list of shared goals.

In fact, over the next few chapters, we'll give you specific details on everything you need to cover money-wise before you get married (or asap, if you're already married)—from merging and managing your money to goal-setting and goal-getting. In the first conversation, though, you don't need to cover all of that. You might feel more comfortable just talking generally about your hopes and dreams, and any financial concerns you have. Then you can get into the nitty-gritty details of your finances in the follow-up discussions.

As you prepare for that first conversation, keep these tips in mind:

- **Choose a comfortable setting.** If you live together, think of the place where you both feel most relaxed outside of the bedroom. (We don't want you falling asleep!) Maybe you enjoy cozying up on the living room couch or sitting together at the kitchen table. If you're the one who is initiating the discussion and you don't live together, suggest having it at his apartment—assuming he doesn't have any roommates or that they'll be out—so that he feels at ease in his surroundings.

- **Cut out the distractions.** Make sure the TV is off. Put away your cellphones and turn off the ringer on the home phone. Make sure your partner won't be focused on other things. If he's a huge hockey fan, for example, the week of the Stanley Cup finals may not be the best time to have this conversation. You don't want to have this discussion over dinner, when you might be focused on food, but rather after the dishes and table have been cleared and cleaned. You may want to share some wine, though, as you talk. (As long as it's not too much wine—you do want to remember this conversation after all.)

- **Agree together on a time.** You don't want to bring this up in the morning before work or right before you head out for an evening, but ensure that you've allotted plenty of time so you don't feel rushed. Nor is it wise to initiate the conversation after he comes home with a big-screen TV and you're livid—just as it wouldn't be a great time for him to launch into the conversation about how careless you are with your money when you've returned from a shoe sale with bags in hand. You want to make sure that neither of you is angry or upset when you start the discussion so that, hopefully, you won't be at the end either.

- **Remember that you're on the same side.** Don't point fingers. Don't get defensive. And try not to rush to judgment. Remember, you want to tackle any financial problems you have as a team. It's important that you offer each other support and encouragement as you share the details of your finances and then look for ways you can help each other, rather than making the other person feel bad about spending too much, saving too little, or not earning enough. Focus on the future, and what you can each do now, rather than on what's happened in the past.

- **Give a little to get a little.** If you volunteer your own fears or feelings about a financial issue, your partner may feel more comfortable doing the same. Be candid about past mistakes—or even current ones—and about any concerns you have, and encourage your partner to do the same. It's not just about coming up with an arrangement that *works* for both of you, but understanding *why* it works for both of you. By being honest about your feelings now, you can prevent either a lot of anger or resentment later on. But you must also be willing to make the changes necessary to address any concerns your partner has and to improve your finances so that you're each doing your part.

- **Stay positive.** Instead of talking about all of the things you think the other person is doing wrong and how misdirected you might be, talk about what you are both doing right and how you can get to your goals even faster by working together. Identify each other's strengths, and use those to figure out how to divvy up your financial responsibilities. Talk generally about the goals that you share and how you can achieve them.

In the coming chapters, we'll help you prioritize those goals and come up with a strategy based on your current situation that can help you reach them even sooner than you may have thought possible.

Smart Cookie Summary

Discussion Questions:

You can ask yourself these questions and keep your responses in a notebook. Or use these to get the conversation started with your partner.

1. Have you ever talked about your finances with your friends and family? Why, or why not?

2. What kinds of money issues have you encountered in past relation-ships? How did you address them?
3. What do you think are your biggest strengths and weaknesses when it comes to managing your money?
4. Looking back, what would you have done differently with your own money?
5. What are some of the benefits you see of managing your finances as a couple?

Smart Steps:

These are steps that you can take yourself, or that you and your partner can do together.

1. Make a list of your own money strengths and weaknesses. Are you good at making money, for example, but have trouble reining in your spending?
2. Make a list of your partner's strengths. Is he (or she) super-organized, for example, or detail oriented? Does he (or she) have a great credit score? These are strengths that can help you determine what roles you're each best suited to play in managing your money. It also helps to remember each other's strengths as you begin your discussion.
3. Make a list of your top five *personal* financial goals. What would you like to improve about your own finances?
4. Make a list of your top five financial goals as a couple. Do you want to be debt free in two years? Do you want to be able to buy a home in three?
5. Bring these lists with you when you sit down to discuss your finances with your partner, and use them to help get the conversation started.

chapter 2

The Baggage We Bring

How Our Money Histories Shape Our Habits

You might not have spent a lot of time talking about money with your parents while you were growing up—but that doesn't mean you weren't learning anything about it from them.

How our parents handle their money—and how they handle the topic itself—has more of an impact on how we deal with our finances as adults than many of us realize. The perspectives and the patterns we develop are often a direct result of observing how our family managed its money and how that affected us growing up.

The *role* that money played in your family also affects how you view it later in life. Maybe money was used as an instrument of control in your household. Or one (or both) of your parents used money as a way to demonstrate their love. Your mom and dad could have used money sparingly or excessively, conscientiously or carelessly, discreetly or ostentatiously—or somewhere in between. Maybe they withheld it when you misbehaved, or until you finished your chores. Or they heaped it on you in an effort to compensate for the time they weren't able to spend with you.

Even if your parents weren't aware of what they were doing, their behaviour may have had a profound effect on the associations you make with money as an adult. If they used money to reward you for good behaviour, for example, you may end up "rewarding" yourself by overspending whenever you need a boost (without realizing you're actually punishing yourself, of course, since you'll end up paying for it in the long run). If one of your parents missed your school plays or hockey games to put in extra hours at work for more pay, you might assume that money was more of a priority than family and resent it, unaware that your parent might have had no choice but to work longer hours in order to pay the bills and keep the roof over your head. Unless your parents talked openly with you about how they made and used their money and the reasons behind their financial decisions—and most don't—you're left to draw your own conclusions from what you observe. And, as we learned, they're not always accurate.

ANGELA'S STORY

Angela's parents are divorced, and until her mother got remarried some years later, she raised both Angela and her brother by herself, working long hours as a nurse. Although Angela now realizes how tough it was for her mother financially, her mother took great pains to shield any money problems from her kids as they were growing up. She grew up in a poor family herself, and wanted to make sure her own kids didn't feel as deprived as she had as a child—even if that meant pulling out the credit card more than she should have. And maybe she was also hoping to compensate for any sense of loss her kids might have felt from the divorce. But by trying so hard to provide everything she could for them and to hide her own financial struggles, Angela's mom inadvertently presented a distorted financial picture to Angela and her brother.

Growing up, Angela says she rarely remembers her mom using cash, just credit cards. "For a long time, I honestly thought that was how you paid for things: with this small piece of plastic. Only years later did I realize that my mom did not have any other means."

Angela's mom has vivid memories of one terminally ill patient who encouraged her to spend her money along the way and enjoy it, as he had not had the chance to do. She admits she took the advice to the extreme, spending every penny she made (usually on her kids). Angela picked up the same habit once she was on her own, spending all of the money she made, and sometimes more, in order to keep up her lifestyle—just as her mother had done for her when she was young. Why save for the future, she thought, when she had so much she wanted to do and have in the present? "I always thought, I'd rather have a great trip with my girlfriends and some great memories, than a pile of money sitting in a retirement account," says Angela. "But now I realize there has to be a balance."

After Angela's mom remarried, she and her new husband worked together to create a plan to pay off the debt, and they did. But Angela didn't fully grasp just how much their former lifestyle had really cost her mother until she became a Smart Cookie and sat down a few years ago with her to have a very frank discussion about it.

Angela's taken steps now to make sure she doesn't fall into the same harmful patterns again by finding a balance between having what she wants now and saving enough to reach her future goals, too.

Some of Katie's happiest memories growing up were the shopping trips that she took with her parents. They made her feel special because her mom and dad lavished both money and attention on her. Not only did she get a chance to spend some time alone with them, but she also got new clothes or toys that she really wanted and didn't have to pay for them. By trying to give her all the things she wanted growing up, though, her parents inadvertently gave her an excuse to justify the many shopping trips she'd later indulge in on her own— when she *did* have to pay for them (and, boy, did she pay!). Katie recalls her dad once telling her that they weren't hurting for money, so if she really, really loved something, there was no reason she shouldn't have it. Once she was on her own, she says she often used that motto to justify her own overspending without even realizing it. She would convince herself that if she really, really loved and wanted something she should have it, even if it required going into debt to get it. Once she became aware of the pattern and the reasons behind it—not to mention the damage it was wreaking on her finances—she became a much savvier shopper and gave herself strict spending limits. It still took her quite a long time to pay off the bills for those shopping trips.

Katie's parents and Angela's mom had only the best intentions. But the messages they inadvertently sent their daughters set them up to be over-spenders once they were on their own.

MEGAN AND DOUG

These stories sound all too familiar to Megan and Doug, a Calgary couple in their 30s who we interviewed. When they first met, both Megan and Doug said they were still in the habit of spending most or all of what they made, and when they sat down later on and talked about their family histories, they understood why. Megan remembers spending the allowance her parents gave her as soon as she got it. But while her parents were responsible with their money, they never talked to her about how she should properly manage her own. Her family might have teased her for spending her allowance so quickly, but because her parents were still covering most of her expenses, Megan didn't fully grasp the conse-quences of spending everything she made without setting anything aside. She had to learn the lesson the hard way once she moved out on her own, after she ran out of cash and ended up with credit card debt.

Doug's parents were fortunate enough to retire early, so growing up he was aware that his family never worried about running out of money—even though neither parent worked. "I now know that the money came from years of hard work, investing, and saving," says Doug. But because his parents didn't explain that to him as a child, he says, he had no clue then that the money was the result of such care-ful planning and steadfast saving. "At the time," he says, "it just seemed to be 'there.'" Of course, once he was on his own, Doug quickly dis-covered what happens when you spend as if more money will always be "there" without actually taking the steps to make sure it is. Like Megan, he ended up with a lot of debt, and anxiety about money that he never experienced growing up. "That debt still weighs on me, and I want to get rid of it as fast as possible," he says. "It prevents me from enjoying the money we have sometimes."

Megan and Doug both realized that because money was always plentiful in their family households, and because their parents had not offered them much detail on how they made and managed their money, they'd each developed some unrealistic beliefs about money. But now that they've learned their lessons, they're much more conscious of how they spend and save their money. Doug now puts more than 20 percent of every paycheque towards his debt, plus any bonus he gets from his job as an IT specialist, and he has diligently been saving more than 10 percent of his pay each month. After Megan recognized the harmful spending patterns she'd been repeating since she was a teenager (when she was fortunate enough to have someone else taking care of her big expenses), she also took steps to ensure she wouldn't go back in debt. She now saves nearly 10 percent of each paycheque. And they're both working towards their future goals.

Under the Influence

Of course, our parents aren't the only ones to influence the way we handle money as adults. We're affected, in varying degrees, by our environment, our peers, and our neighbours, too—and by society's expectations of the roles we'll play as adults. Even our gender can be a factor in how we're taught to approach money. Though women have made huge strides in the workplace, many of us are still raised to be nurturers and caregivers, roles that emphasize our compassionate and charitable qualities, but not necessarily our money-making or money-managing abilities. Growing up, we often learn how to spend our money, on ourselves and on those we care about, but *not* how to save or invest it.

A survey by the Charles Schwab Foundation, conducted just a few years ago, found that teenaged girls are still much more likely than teenaged boys to get their money from credit or debit cards (43 percent versus just 26 percent) and also much more likely to be in debt (40 percent versus 23 percent). While they are more knowledgeable about writing a cheque and using a credit card than their male counterparts, teen girls also report being less interested in learning more about saving and investing.

It's no wonder, then, that researchers have found that adult women make the majority of the spending decisions in the household yet they often take a backseat when it comes to investing. Men, meanwhile, are often trained to be providers. They're not just encouraged to fend for themselves but to be prepared to support a wife and maybe a family, too (even if they don't end up doing so). Obviously, that doesn't mean they'll all grow up to be models of fiscal responsibility or that they'll never overspend. But many are taught to save their money and invest it, too, not just to spend it. Even if they have debt, as Doug did, they also tend to have savings and investment accounts.

Of course, these are generalizations and there are exceptions. But it's worth exploring whether any reluctance you have to invest, or ambivalence you have about saving your money, may have something to do with the role *you* were encouraged to fill as well as the role money played in your family.

The Meaning of Money

If you're subconsciously sabotaging your efforts at financial success, it may also be a result of the way you view money itself. As we said, the experience we have with money growing up not only affects our spending habits but also the way we actually think about money as adults. If your dad was always complaining about "the greedy rich," for example, you're likely to link the two words in your mind as well, and it could even keep you from pursuing wealth yourself. Of course, you have the power to change any ideas you have about money that might be holding you back from making more. But first, you must become aware of those thoughts.

Look up the word "money" in the dictionary, and you'll see it described simply as "a medium of exchange" or "a means of payment." But that definition doesn't take into account the associations we give to money, whether consciously or not. Some people equate it with love, others with power or status. Some see money as synonymous with security; others associate it with anxiety. Those ideas can be based partly on the interactions we had with those we perceived as having a lot of money. They are also influenced by what our parents did with their money, as well as the role it played in our lives as we were growing up—whether it was scarce or plentiful, a source of stress or of celebration, something to be feared or to be revered.

Since you and your partner each had unique experiences growing up, it's quite possible that you have very different views on the role money should play in your lives. Don't worry, this can actually be beneficial; you can learn from each other. But in order to do that, you need to talk about it.

And remember that ultimately money is just a means by which to achieve the life you both want. That's something you should be able to agree on. Whatever associations and experiences you might have had with money in the past, you really want to focus now on making it work for you in the future.

What's Your Money Type?

As we've explained in this chapter, the daily decisions we make about money are often driven by psychological factors that we may not even be aware of—biases, beliefs, and behaviour patterns we've picked up from our parents and our peers, as well as our emotions and our environments. All of these factors influence the way we approach money and help to determine the type of money manager we'll become.

Are you nervous about investing in anything that might lose value? Do you like to take calculated risks, knowing that the payoff could be much higher than if you played it safe? Do you like to treat yourself to some new clothes when you get a bonus? Or put it directly into your savings? Is it important to you to look successful—even if it means using some of your savings in order to buy that sports car or that designer bag?

How you answer these questions can give you some insight into the type of money personality you've developed as an adult. It will affect the way you approach a variety of issues related to money. (It may also explain why you and your partner often disagree on how to handle some of those issues.) Want to find out more about what type you are? Read through the statements below and circle the number that best applies to you. Then add up your score to find out what money personality you most identify with. You may find that you've got aspects of more than one money type. Pay attention to any description for which you had three or more responses, then discuss your responses with your partner. You may be surprised by what you learn.

1. When it comes to managing my money:

A) I'm careful to be sure all the bills are paid and that there's always plenty in my savings account.

B) I just do my best to make sure I always earn enough to stay ahead.

C) I usually "manage" to spend most—if not all—of it before the next cheque comes.

D) I try, but with varying levels of success. I just don't care that much about money.

E) I am a fanatic, devoting hours each month to making sure I'm on track to reach my goals.

F) I don't.

2. When I actually have savings:

A) I put all or most of it immediately into a money market or savings account.

B) I like to use some of it, at least, to splurge on something expensive.

C) I spend it immediately.

D) I keep some and give the rest away to worthy causes or needy friends.

E) I do some research to find the highest-yielding bank account or CDs (an interest-paying investment certificate), then put it there.

F) I keep it in my sock drawer or stash it somewhere in the house for when I need it.

3. I pay my bills:

A) In full and often well before they are due so I don't risk falling behind or missing a payment.

B) On time, though sometimes I carry a small balance.

C) As quickly as I can, but it's hard to keep up with all of them!

D) Most often on time, but occasionally I fall behind when I'm focused on other things.

E) Diligently, reviewing each statement carefully for potential errors, fees, or rate increases.

F) When I think of it. But I often lose track of whether I've paid them all or not.

4. Credit card debt is:

A) Something I never want to have. I try to avoid even using a credit card.

B) Sometimes necessary to support my goals, but I know I'll eventually be able to pay it all off.

C) A part of life.

D) A waste. I'd rather give my money to charity than to the credit card companies.

E) Too costly. If I use my card, I pay the balance off immediately to avoid any interest charges.

F) A bummer, especially since I got hit with a late fee and my interest rate jumped to 25 percent!

5. I plan to retire:

    A) By 65, if I invest carefully. But I don't plan to live extravagantly.

    B) As soon as I can afford to stop working yet maintain a luxurious lifestyle.

    C) At some point, but why think about that now? I'm too busy enjoying life!

    D) After I've set enough aside to live on, and then spend most of my time volunteering.

    E) Very well, and I adjust my portfolio every year to make sure I am on track to reach my goal.

    F) When I'm old. But I can't be bothered to worry about that yet.

6. Becoming wealthy:

    A) Would be nice. But I just want to be sure I've got enough in the bank for my family to get by comfortably.

    B) Will definitely happen for me, but I also want to enjoy the ride getting there.

    C) Is less important to me than just enjoying life now.

    D) Isn't really a goal, though it'd be nice to give money to the causes I care about.

    E) Is my ultimate goal.

    F) Ain't gonna happen unless I win the lottery.

7. If I was invited on a vacation I would:

    A) Save up until I had enough cash to pay for it in full.

    B) Find a way to make extra money outside of my job to make the trip happen.

    C) Not think twice about it. Can we upgrade to first class?

    D) Think first about what else I could use that money for to help family or friends.

E) Go, but likely opt out of any upgrades or costly extras, and see if I could find a way to expense some of it.

F) Probably forget about it. It's not worth working extra hours to afford it when I'd probably be just as happy spending my holiday at home with my friends.

8. If I was in the market to buy a house, I'd:

A) Look for something I could afford to put 20 percent down on and live in for the long term.

B) Stretch myself a bit on the mortgage payments if I found something I loved, feeling confident that I could make it work.

C) Go to the top of my financial limit, even I risked getting in over my head. Having the nicest house on the block is worth it.

D) Look for a home that I know my family and friends would like and be able to enjoy as well.

E) Look at it like an investment, putting a priority on finding a home that had good resale value.

F) I'll likely be renting forever.

HOW TO SCORE

If your answers were mainly A, you identify most with:
Security Seekers. These types tend to be very averse to risk, and seek out mostly conservative investments and money strategies—occasionally to their own detriment. They are comfortable living on less because they'd rather be safe than sorry when it comes to their money and investments. Pros: They avoid overspending and are good savers. They invest conservatively and don't often lose money. Cons: They may miss out on big returns as well. They also tend to be average earners and take the path of least resistance. They don't usually get rich, but they're not likely to end up poor either.

If your answers were mainly B, you identify most with:

Achievers. These types tend to be quite ambitious and very aware of their status. Their motto: Work hard, play hard. If they have the money, they're not afraid to spend it, often opting for expensive, flashy purchases that will show others just how "successful" they are. They are willing to take major, calculated financial risks. Pros: They are ambitious and tend to earn a lot, and are confident in their money-making abilities. Cons: Taking a risk can sometimes lead to big losses. And the "work hard, play hard" mentality can create a lifestyle that is hard to keep up.

If your answers were mainly C, you identify most with:

High Rollers. These types are really focused on living the high life. They're pleasure- and thrill-seekers and they like to have fun, no matter what the cost. Their motto: Let the good times roll! They often make money, but they're quick to spend it, too, on themselves and those around them. Pros: They're not averse to risk, which can potentially be a good thing. They are fun to be around and generous with others. Cons: They tend to overspend and accumulate debt. They aren't usually great savers and often underestimate how much they should be putting into their retirement funds. (They're too focused on the here and now.)

If your answers were mainly D, you identify most with:

Idealists. Money is less important to these types. They're more focused on what they can do with their money to help others and better the world, than on actually *making* money. They're optimists and believe things will always work out. Pros: They don't tend to spend their money frivolously. They are kind-hearted and generous, and try to use their money for good. Cons: Their lack of interest in personal finance details means they're not great money managers. While they don't tend to overspend, they also don't tend to be great earners. And they can be so focused on helping others that they forget about helping themselves—not setting enough aside in savings, for example, for their retirement.

If your answers were mainly E, you identify most with:

Systematic Strivers. These types like to consider all of their options before they make any financial decisions—major or minor. They enjoy doing research and looking at the facts and figures, and then taking the course of action they think will make the most sense financially. But that can sometimes come at the expense of other benefits. They might take a job with a higher paycheque, for example, over one that could potentially be more satisfying but doesn't pay well. Pros: Many aspects of their skills and focus can make them great money managers: They're not likely to overspend or to have debt (it just doesn't add up), and they usually have more than adequate savings and a well-balanced portfolio of investments. Cons: Paralysis by analysis. Sometimes they get so caught up in weighing every detail that they can have trouble actually making a decision. They may also be so focused on the financial result that they overlook intangible rewards that are harder to measure, which could ultimately result in a decision that leaves them frustrated or unfulfilled.

If your answers were mainly F, you identify most with:

Dawdlers. These slacker types are well-intentioned but, when it comes down to it, they just can't be bothered to take an active role in their finances. They're perpetual procrastinators. They often forget to pay their bills, or fall behind simply because they never got around to it. Pros: They're not typically big spenders, neither on themselves nor on others, and don't need material items to define who they are. In fact, they probably prefer to sit at home in old, ratty sweats, watching TV, eating pizza, and drinking cheap beer, than to get dressed up and eat out at a fancy restaurant. Cons: They don't pay attention to their finances, so they often fall behind on their bills and obligations. Not only can this hurt their credit score, but they may end up paying hundreds of dollars more in interest and late charges. They're also more likely to opt for convenience, which often costs more (think of the convenience store versus the discount centre and paid parking that's close versus free parking that requires a walk). They're not typically big earners either because they would rather not put the effort into making more.

Remember that your money personality can be a combination of these types, as long as at least three of your answers matched the category. In fact, it's likely that you'll relate to aspects of more than one of the descriptions. Still, many of you will find that you identify most closely with one in particular—and it may not be the same one your partner does. Again, that's okay. The important thing is to become aware of what your tendencies are with money; it will help you both to fight against your weaknesses and take advantage of your strengths.

Now that you've read about Doug's aversion to debt *and* completed the quiz yourself, you're probably not surprised to hear that he scored high as a Security Seeker. His wife, Megan, meanwhile, identified most closely with the Achiever type. These two types can complement each other, but their differing tendencies can also lead to conflict if they're not careful: Security Seekers like to save their money and invest conservatively, while Achievers tend to spend more and to take more risks with their money. Megan may find that she has to convince Doug to take more calculated risks with their money, and thinks that he should splurge occasionally on something he really wants. And Doug will need to help Megan fight her tendencies to overspend. If they can find that balance, both their finances and their marriage will benefit.

Stephanie and Eric, a married couple with two young kids who we interviewed in San Francisco, both scored highest as Security Seekers. Stephanie wasn't surprised at all by her results. She remembers marveling as a preteen about a next-door neighbour in Dallas (where she grew up) whose parents had a boat and two sports cars, and had installed a large swimming pool with a water slide in their backyard. At first, Stephanie was envious. But her neighbour's father worked in the oil industry and when the market crashed in the 1980s, the boat and the cars disappeared. Then the "For Sale" sign appeared in the front yard. Stephanie's father explained that her neighbours had spent all their money on luxury items that made them look rich, but they didn't have enough savings, so when the father lost his job and their investments went south, they found themselves in serious financial trouble. They were forced to sell off all those items they'd bought when times were good, and move into a smaller house in a different neighbourhood. The lesson had a powerful effect on Stephanie, who always saved some of the allowance she got as a teenager, and avoided taking on any credit card debt as an adult. In fact, she can recall just one time in her life that she carried a credit card balance, and it was only for a month. Though she and her husband earn good salaries as a doctor and engineer, respectively, she says she still needs to have a financial cushion for her peace of mind: enough money so that the family would be okay for at least six months if either she or her husband lost their jobs.

Stephanie was initially surprised that Eric scored equally high in the Security Seeker category, because she remembers when he racked up nearly $5,000 in credit card debt shortly after they got together. But Eric was quick to reminded her that he hasn't carried a penny of balance since he paid it off. Lesson learned. While he's more apt to spend his personal money more freely than she does, he's still always been able to set aside enough for any of their short-term goals.

Stephanie says it was comforting to see that they were so similar. Knowing that they're both reluctant to spend their savings or put their money into risky investments gives her faith that they'll be able to budget for their big goals, and reach them. And she doesn't have to worry about either of them putting the family into a precarious position. In fact, when she and Eric bought their first home, they both agreed to look in a range that was $50,000 to $100,000 *below* the maximum the bank was willing to lend them because they didn't want to overextend themselves. As a result, they were able to save money even as they made their mortgage payments. And then they made enough on the sale of their first house to set money aside for a good down payment on their next one. Even though they can afford to buy a bigger home now, they're renting while they save up enough to make a 20-percent down payment on the kind of home they want, something they both agreed on.

Like Security Seekers, Systematic Strivers are wary of taking on debt or putting themselves into a position that might jeopardize their financial success, and they can serve as an effective counterweight against a partner's tendency to overspend or to overlook financial details. In turn, of course, they may need to be reminded that it's okay to spend money sometimes on small indulgences or in ways that offer intrinsic but not necessarily *monetary* rewards. When Katie and her husband, Nick, took the quiz, she scored highest as an Achiever, while he identified most with the Systematic Striver. Their responses offered each of them insight into the other's financial decisions and tendencies. Katie realized that her husband's investment recommendations weren't necessarily conservative, but they were carefully researched. She also realized that while she thought of herself as having more of an analytic approach to money, her bursts of spending could stem from pressure to keep up her appearance in her role as founder of a PR firm (and before that, a PR manager). On the other hand, even when she didn't have a formal plan, Katie has always strived to increase her earnings—she even started her own consulting firm while still working full-time. In the case of Katie and Nick, their money type combination has been very lucrative. They're both big earners, and they are willing to take well-researched, calculated risks that have so far paid off for them. Nick helps to keep Katie's spending impulses in check, and Katie helps Nick to remember to have fun along the way, even as they work towards their bigger goals. "We both appreciate how we balance one another," says Katie.

That's the ultimate goal. By recognizing what your strengths are, you can take advantage of them. And by identifying your financial weaknesses, you can help each other overcome them. Then you'll be able to enjoy the financial benefits that come with being part of a strong partnership. Any combination of type can work, as long as you are committed to similar goals. (Although if you're with a Dawdler, you may need to ask yourself whether he or she will ever make the effort that's required to reach your financial goals.)

We encourage you to identify and discuss your money types and histories, so you know the reasons behind some of the patterns you've developed individually as adults, and can help each other avoid falling into the habits that might keep you from reaching your goals. But it's also important to be clear about your values, so you know what is truly important to each other. In order to have the life you really want, you need to make sure you're also aligning your money practices with your values as a couple. You may each have different values that are most important to you, so you want to make sure that you come up with a financial plan that encompasses all of them.

HOW DO YOU VALUE MONEY?

Take a look at the following list of values. Now, write down three to four of the values below that are really important to you now, in order of importance, and ask your partner to do the same. (No peeking!)

Security	Family/Marriage
Freedom	Charity
Independence	Creativity
Happiness	Culture
Peace of mind	Fulfillment
Fun	Personal growth
Excitement	Balance
Adventure	Health/Wellness
Power	Community involvement
Status	Legacy/Purpose
Influence	

Now think of one or two ways you could achieve each of your top values. If security is important to you, for example, what steps would you want to take as a couple to feel more secure financially? What about having a year's worth of living expenses in the bank? Or being completely debt free? Or, let's say fun is a top priority: What activities would you like to be able to do in order to have more fun? Would you like to spend three weeks travelling each year? Do you want to take up skydiving or skiing? If having balance in your life is really critical, what would you need to change in order to achieve that? Would you like to work part-time instead of full-time, or just find a more flexible job? Would finding balance mean spending more quality time with your family or with your friends? Travelling more? Or finding a way to incorporate more activities like yoga and meditation into your life? Write down whatever comes to mind next to the values you've listed. Then talk to your partner.

Don't worry if you haven't listed the same values. As we mentioned earlier, it's likely that you won't have the same top priorities.

What's most important again is that you talk about them, respect each other's choices, and find areas where they overlap. As you move forward through this book, you want to keep all of the values you listed in mind. They'll help you to prioritize some of the financial goals you'll be outlining in Chapter Four. And they should also be reflected in the spending plan you create in Chapter Five.

But for now, we just want to get you thinking about them and talking about them with your partner. It's essential that you not just recognize the values that really matter to you, but that you understand what values your partner ranks high on his (or her) list. After all, how can you create a future together if you don't know what's most important to each of you? If you don't take the time to sort out what each of you wants in life, you may end up creating a life that doesn't make you happy. But if you're clear about what's important to each other, you can start redirecting your money and your energy towards those areas of your lives and create a future that makes you both happy.

Smart Cookie Summary

Discussion Questions:

1. What role did money play in your life when you were growing up?
2. How do you think your parents approached money?
3. Did you ever talk about money with your parents? If yes, what can you recall about those conversations?
4. What money type do you identify with most strongly?
5. What four values are most important to you now?

Smart Steps:

1. Set aside some time for each of you to talk about your money histories.
2. Write down three ways in which you think your parents influenced the way you approach money. Discuss them with your partner.
3. Ask your parents what financial advice they wish they'd given you, or what advice they'd give you now.
4. Take the money personality quiz with your partner and discuss the results.
5. Identify your top values from the list above, and discuss your choices with your partner.

chapter 3

Do You See What I See?

Planning Your Perfect Day Together

When we formed the Smart Cookies Money Club, one of the first discussions we had wasn't even specifically about money. Instead, we spent an entire meeting talking about what each of us wanted our lives to look like in five years. Would we be living in the same apartments or in new homes, and who might be sharing them with us? Where did we want to be career-wise? How would we like to be spending our days and evenings? We set aside all of our money concerns for a few hours and just allowed ourselves to imagine the lives we hoped to have.

You might wonder why we took the time to fantasize about our futures instead of focusing on the money problems we were meeting to solve. The answer is simple: for inspiration. Because we needed to be reminded of the reasons *why* we wanted to improve our finances and what we were working so hard to achieve. Without a clear idea of what we were each making and saving money for, we knew it would be much tougher—if not impossible—to stay on track.

Figuring out where you and your partner stand right now *is* important. But if you're planning on spending your future together, you also need to spend some time talking about what kind of future you want it to be. Envisioning your lives a few years down the road will give you both a clearer picture of the kind of life you want to create *together,* so you can start taking the steps you need to get there. Don't worry if your visions aren't exactly the same. That doesn't mean you aren't meant to be together. It just means that it's even more important for you to discuss what's really important to each of you individually and as a couple—and what's not. You need to be able to create a picture of your future together in which you both fit comfortably—one that will make you happy and motivate you to earn and save more money so you can make it a reality that much sooner.

To help get you started, try the exercise below. You may each want to take some time alone to read and answer the questions and then get together to discuss your responses. You can also get the questions online at www.smartcookies.com.

Picturing Your Perfect Day Together

Set any money problems you're dealing with now aside for a moment and ask yourself: What do you *want* your life to look like in five years? Close your eyes and imagine it's a Friday morning five years from now. Or a Wednesday or a Tuesday. (We suggest you choose a weekday—rather than a weekend—so it can involve the kind of work you want to be doing.) What would make it your perfect day? You can use the questions below to help walk you through the exercise, but feel free to come up with your own, too.

1. What time do you wake up?
2. Where do you live? (Go into detail: Are you by the water or mountains? On an island? Are you in a big city or a small suburb? What does your home look like? Downtown loft or rambling country home?)
3. Who is with you? (Are you married? Do you have children? Pets? Is your family nearby?)
4. What kind of work are you doing, where, and with whom? Have you achieved your career goals yet? Are you on the right track?
5. As you head out to face the day, how do you look? What are you wearing? (Have your priorities changed?)

6. What is your daily work schedule like and how do you get there? Or do you work from home? What do you drive? (Or do you walk or bike?)

7. When your workday is over, how do you spend the rest of your day—and with whom?

8. How do you spend your evening? (Where are you? What are you eating and drinking? What activities are you doing? Who's with you?)

9. How would you spend any time alone? Is "alone-time" important to you?

10. When you look back on the day, what are you most grateful for?

11. As you drift off to sleep, what are you looking forward to doing in the coming days?

Allow yourself to imagine all the possibilities. Don't let credit card debt, or a dwindling bank balance, keep you from envisioning the future you truly want. This should be a clear snapshot of life *exactly* as you'd want it to be with your partner or spouse, if you were no longer worried about money.

In the space below the description you've written down, answer these questions:

• **Which five activities that you participate in on your perfect day bring you the most joy?** These can include doing work you love or meditating in the morning, or less structured things like playing with your children, walking to work, or cooking dinner for your spouse. What kinds of sports do you like doing? What are your favourite pastimes? What's your ideal job? It's your perfect day. You can spend it doing anything you'd like, regardless of the cost.

• **What are five things you envisioned in your perfect day that you don't already have?** Any five things. From a new baby and a Volvo station wagon to a vacation home or a golf club membership to toned biceps or an RRSP.

Whatever you want to have on your perfect day should be included in your plan, no matter how far-fetched it may seem to you now. Include as many details as you can, so you can truly imagine how your life would look if you had everything you wanted.

Angela pictured herself sharing strawberry daiquiris (her favourite) with her boyfriend, or husband, and family on a deck outside a custom-built lake-front vacation cottage that she'd helped purchase. Andrea imagined living in a brownstone apartment in Manhattan, vacationing at an oceanfront home she'd bought in Cape Cod, Massachusetts, and working in a job that allowed her to travel frequently to see her family and friends in Canada. In Robyn's perfect day, she was married with kids, a dog, and a flexible job. She was living in a dream home that she and her husband had designed together, complete with a gourmet kitchen, oversized living room, and a wraparound porch. Katie saw herself in a beautiful, spacious home with her husband and two kids, cooking dinner on state-of-the-art appliances for her family and close friends. Nick envisioned having a gold club membership, a home with a big lawn where their two kids could play, and a vacation cottage. (We'll give you more details on how Katie and Nick combined their perfect day goals later in the chapter.)

Don't be worried if your partner doesn't come up with the same perfect day as you—as long as you're in it! In fact, it's unlikely you'll both come up with exactly the same descriptions and activities. The important thing is that your visions of the future are compatible and that you can agree on some of the major decisions, like where you want to live and whether you see kids in your future. If you're picturing a day with children and he (or she) is not, then you need to have a serious chat about your priorities and determine whether it's a question of adjusting your timelines or your expectations. If you have drasti-cally different ideas of where you'll be living, you should ask yourselves what it is exactly that you're looking for in your home and your surroundings. What appealed to you about the home and area you described in the exercise? Could you find a different place that has all the qualities you're seeking? Can you come up with a compromise?

When one of the couples we interviewed did this exercise, they initially came up with very different descriptions for their perfect home. Doug, an IT specialist in Calgary, envisioned a lakefront home with a dock, while his wife, Megan, a schoolteacher, pictured them in a traditional suburban house just outside the city. So they compromised: They'd get a home in the suburbs, at least while they raised a family, but they'd also own or rent a vacation cottage on the lake. Then once their kids grew up and moved out, they could move into that home on the lake that Doug dreamed about, and maybe even buy a boat to tie up to their dock. Rather than give up their visions of their perfect homes, they found a way to incorporate both of them in different ways and at different stages in their lives.

Often, couples will realize that they have similar goals but different time-lines. Maybe one of you assumed you'd start a family right away, while the other planned to wait a few more years to build a nest egg first. What should you do? Take it one step at a time. Maybe start by discussing the minimum amount you each feel you need to have saved in order to feel prepared financially to raise a child. Once you agree on a figure, focus on finding ways to save that money faster so that you can start a family sooner. (We'll give you ideas in the coming chapters.) This way you're taking both of your goals into consideration, and providing a powerful incentive to work harder now to save that extra money.

The Perfect Day exercise is really intended to get you both thinking and talking about the life you want to create together, and to inspire and motivate you to start taking the necessary steps to make it happen. So as a couple, you should ultimately agree on a snapshot of your future *together* that you can both get excited about. But as you discuss the reasons behind the choices you made for your perfect day, you may decide to adjust some of your timelines, goals, or priorities so that they're better aligned with your partner's. That's what happened with Katie and Nick.

KATIE AND NICK

Each of our personal goals had a heavy focus on career and on getting ahead financially. But after doing the Perfect Day exercise together and discussing our values, we both wanted to make spending quality time together a priority as well. And we also acknowledged how important family was. Yes, we still wanted the six-figure income and the dream home, but we decided that it was equally as important to try and create a balance between our work and our personal lives. We wanted to spend more time together, so we decided to put off buying a new home in order to set aside the savings we needed to start a family, and to scale back our pace at work a bit so we would have more time together before we started having kids.

For me, that meant taking on fewer projects, and sacrificing a little income from my PR business so I wouldn't spend all my spare time working or even thinking about work. It was hard for me at first, but it was worth it. Nick and I were able to start doing some of the activities we had always talked about, but never had time for. Now we make the time. We go to art galleries and museums, we rock climb together and have even taken a couples cooking class. We also realize that these experiences have helped to strengthen our marriage more than the extra income. We're still earning enough to feel comfortable that we can reach our future goals, but we're a lot less stressed out, and we're able to spend more time together doing the things we love.

CLAIRE AND RYAN

Claire and Ryan, a married couple in their 30s who we interviewed in Toronto, completed the Perfect Day exercise, listed several goals that related to their responses, and then went through their lists together to decide as a couple what would be a priority in the short term. This way they both felt that they were involved in deciding what to focus on. Prioritizing their goals together also helped them figure out how much they should each be saving now and exactly how that money would be spent. They decided that paying down the mortgage, saving for retirement, and saving for their newborn daughter's education were their top three financial goals, and immediately began sorting out how to accomplish them. Both Claire and Ryan were willing to postpone some of their individual goals in the short term—like working half days, or finding a job that would cut the commute—to focus first on those goals they shared.

They set up a monthly meeting to keep track of the progress they'd made, discuss any challenges that had come up in the interim, and to decide whether they wanted to make any changes to their list. "It was really a matter of shifting the focus from our individual lives to our life together. We weren't giving up our personal goals, just shifting our priorities," says Claire. "Realizing we were both making our family life a priority made it much easier to plan for the future together."

Doing this exercise at one of our early Smart Cookies meetings also prompted each of us to take a hard look at where our money was then going and whether it was helping us reach our goals, or holding us back. Each of us made some immediate changes in the way we saved and spent our money after seeing how the choices we were making then did, or didn't, fit into the bigger plans we had for our lives.

When we first did this exercise, for example, Sandra told us she wanted to own a loft apartment downtown, work with friends in a job with a flexible schedule, and have most evenings free to enjoy good wine, food, and music with a boyfriend (or husband) and her closest friends and family. After she'd finished sharing the details of her perfect day, she realized how starkly different that vision was from her life at that point.

Now, in less than two years, Sandra has come a lot closer to living that perfect day she described to us. She has since paid off her credit card debt and set aside more than $15,000 to put towards a down payment, and while she saves up more, she's rented a loft apartment in the same downtown neighbourhood where she plans to buy. She still takes on contract work, but she left her full-time corporate PR job to focus on the Smart Cookies business. So she is now working with friends (that'd be the four of us) and has a much more flexible schedule. And, since she no longer has to work late at the office—something she often did in her previous job—most of her evenings are now free to enjoy good wine, meals, and music with her closest friends and family—and meet new people. Sandra's new boyfriend appreciates gourmet pizza, a good cut of pork, and a nice merlot as much as she does—and even shares her taste in country music!

One of the other advantages of envisioning your perfect day is that it reminds you—or should, anyway—that you are in control of your own financial destiny. Even if you each owe thousands of dollars to your creditors, have no savings to speak of, and make less than you'd like to in your jobs, it's not too late to turn your situation around. Your financial goals are still well within your reach. And you can likely achieve them a lot sooner than you think, especially since you'll be working as a team. The fact that you've bought this book means you're already committed to taking steps to improve your finances. Stay confident and focused, and you *will* get there together—no matter how ambitious it may seem right now—just by continuing in the same direction, one step at a time. It's okay if your goals seem a little intimidating right now. Trust us: At the time each of us came up with our perfect days, we weren't quite sure if they'd ever happen, either (Sandra included). But as we created our spending plans and changed our behaviour, we actually started to see some real changes. Within months, each of us had already made significant strides towards achieving the goals we'd written down—by ourselves and with our partners. We'll help you do the same. It really is possible to live your perfect day within the next five years.

Keep in mind that as you're planning your future, it's also essential to remember the positive things in your life right now. Even if your financial situation isn't exactly what you want it to be, we're sure there's a lot you both have to be grateful for in your life. We don't want you to be so focused on having a better future that you get frustrated with your life today. This isn't about finding a quick fix, but about developing a new outlook on your finances and your financial prospects and adopting and nurturing the kinds of behaviours and strategies that you will benefit from for the rest of your life. And being grateful for what you already have now—a supportive partner, for one—is a great start.

Improve Your Vision

In order to keep motivated, we thought we should do more than just imagine and write down descriptions of our perfect days, so we also created "vision boards" to remind us of what we want to have in our lives and the goals we want to accomplish. You've probably heard of them: Oprah Winfrey has talked about them on her show. They're usually posters or bulletin boards you cover with a collage of inspiring words, phrases, and images. A vision board is a very personal thing: It can include photographs of people you love or admire; inspirational words and images you've cut out of magazines; a brochure or a postcard depicting a destination you want to visit; or a keychain to symbolize the car you want to own. You can add anything that will remind you of your goals and help motivate you to stay on track.

We've found that creating these boards can really help you keep your goals in mind so you're less tempted to spend money in ways that will delay or distract you from reaching them. Still, we do understand that not everyone has the time or interest to take on this project. Some of you may even find the concept, well, a little cheesy. (What *Bachelor* fan doesn't remember the ribbing that Renee, the L.A. jewellery designer, took when she shared her vision board with Jason Mesnick in the first episode of the 2009 season.)

You don't have to create an elaborate vision board to enjoy the benefits it can bring. If you see an ad for that dream car, cut it out and stick it on your fridge. If you read an article about a place where you'd love to vacation together, clip and save it. If you spot that perfect home during a drive one day, take a picture of it and keep it on your camera. You can even start a folder of anything that reminds you of the perfect day you're striving for—or just stick it in a drawer. The idea is just to give yourselves a visual reminder of your goals.

Instead of creating a collage, Katie suggested her husband Nick should start writing out a list of 101 life goals. They came up with 50 goals apiece initially. But in the weeks since they first started, they've both expanded their lists. Nick's goals range from working out three times a week and taking a carpentry class to buying a summer cottage and having two kids. Katie posted her list on her vision board. It included goals like learning a second language and buying a home large enough to accommodate several overnight guests. They still add to their lists, even as they tick off the goals they've reached. Katie's latest addition was having a walk-in closet. So when they look at houses now, that's become one of the criteria. They also compared their lists to help come up with the three big short-term goals that they both wanted, then created a specific plan to achieve them over the next several months. We'll show you how they did it a little later in this chapter, and how much progress they've made.

Sandra and her boyfriend, Jason, are using a digital picture frame as their vision board. They use it to display rotating digital images of the people, experiences, and places that they want to be a part of their future. The initial lineup includes photos of him playing golf, to represent the golf club he wants to join, and images they've pulled of Hawaii and other destinations they plan to visit together. Sandra's also come up with her own 101 life goals. After sharing them with her boyfriend, he actually helped her scratch one off her list by surprising her with tickets to the hockey playoffs. (She'd always dreamed of seeing a playoff game live.)

Visualizing your perfect day and the specific items and activities you want to be a part of that day are also important because once you have a clear idea of what truly brings you joy, you'll have a better idea of what *doesn't*. So you'll be less susceptible to sales pitches or advertisements for products you don't really need that could suck up your savings and slow the progress towards your goals. Marketers want you to imagine a better life that incorporates their clients' products and, often, they're successful. That's why companies pay so much to place their products in popular TV shows and to create commercials depicting lifestyles they think viewers will aspire to emulate (lifestyles that include their brands, of course). If you don't take the time to visualize the smart S bite

TEST DRIVE YOUR DREAMS. Want to make your goals seem even more real? After you cut out photos of your dream car, go to a dealership and spend an afternoon test driving it. You can do the same with your dream home. Spend a weekend afternoon with a Realtor® or real estate agent looking at potential homes and take photos of the one you want, then add them to your board (or stick them into a folder or on the fridge). Seek out someone who's doing your dream job and take them for coffee. If you have the money, check out vocationvacations.com. It's a website that can set you up to spend a day, or a week, getting mentored by experts in a range of interesting and enviable jobs (for a fee, of course)—from a baseball team owner or dogsled trainer to a scriptwriter, a luthier, or a winemaker. Making your dreams more tangible is an excellent way to inspire and motivate yourself. And it will also give you a chance to make sure that the goals you've listed are truly the ones that you want, and to make any adjustments.

kind of life you truly want—one that's based on your *own* values, goals, and interests—then marketers will be only too happy to create that image for you.

Retailers aren't the only ones who may urge you to make decisions that aren't in your best interest. If you don't make it clear that you're trying to save money or pay off your debt, your friends or colleagues may (unwittingly) encourage you to spend the money that you could be putting towards those goals on an expensive meal out, say, or a pair of pants that you don't really need. If you know what kind of house you want but you aren't certain about where you want to live, and the kind of amenities you want to live near, a Realtor® may steer you towards a neighbourhood or a home that isn't really a good fit. Unless you are sure about your career path and go after the salary you think you deserve, your boss has every reason to put off promotions and pay you as little as he or she can to save money. If you don't think about the position you want in your company or the ultimate career you hope to have and plan accordingly, your boss is going to put you in a role that serves his or her best interest but not necessarily yours. Even your closest friends and family may unintentionally push you into making decisions that lead you away from what you truly want, if you don't identify and share your goals. They may think they know what's best for you or may simply want you to help them feel better about the decisions they've made (like urging you to splurge on something to make them feel less guilty about doing it themselves). If you want to reach your goals, you need to know what they are and speak up about them. Not only does that encourage those who care about you to do what they can to help you make them a reality, but the more you talk about your goals the more real they become. And we're not just talking about financial goals. The Perfect Day exercise should help you both think about what you want in *every* aspect of your lives, not just in your bank account, so you can start taking steps together to get there.

Once you're both clear on what your goals are and what you need from each other and from your loved ones in order to reach them, they can help you. In fact, your loved ones may end up helping in ways you might not have even imagined. Maybe you've told them that you're saving for a home, working to pay off your debt, and setting some money aside so you can start a family. You might find out that a family member has a close friend who's a Realtor® who can give you a heads-up on homes that are going up for sale in the neighbourhood you love. Maybe a relative will offer to help pay off some of your debt or give you an interest-free loan to pay off the balance, so you're at least saving money on the interest. (Just make sure you pay him or her back promptly!) If you're pregnant, your friends can throw you a baby shower so you can get many of the items you need for your baby's room for free. Friends with kids might also have clothes, toys, even baby carriers or strollers that their children have outgrown that they'd be happy to give or lend to you, potentially saving you hundreds of dollars. By sharing your goals with those around you they can support you in a number of ways, and also help to hold you accountable. You might even inspire them to start planning their own perfect days.

Of course, if you and your partner had the money to live *your* perfect day now, you probably wouldn't be reading this book. So the next step is to determine what's standing between you and the life you both want. Is it credit card debt, a lack of savings, or an income issue? Over the next few chapters, we'll help you tackle whatever it is that's keeping you from getting there now. But in order to figure out how much you both need to adjust your spending, savings, and earnings, you'll need to put a price tag on some of those perfect day priorities.

After you've discussed the items and activities that you each listed in the Perfect Day exercise, narrow it down to five-ish things that you want to focus on first. Next to each goal, write down approximately how much money you think you'll need to achieve it. This may require a little research. If it's something like a Mercedes convertible that you want, look up the sticker price for the model you want or visit a dealership. (Of course, you can also look for a pre-owned model in the classifieds or dealerships, if you want to cut the cost so you can have it sooner.) If you and your partner would like to take a two-week vacation together each year to some exotic destination, pick a couple spots, plan your itinerary, and then price it out. Don't forget to take into account things like luggage, visas, and exchange rates. If you both have dreams of buying a four-bedroom home in a specific neighbourhood, check your local real estate listings or call a real estate agent. If you want to have a baby, do a little research to find out how much child care costs in your city, and how much you'd need to pay for the basics in your baby's nursery. Several sites offer checklists of what you'll need for a baby, including www.babycenter.ca and www.canadianparents.com. You can also estimate prices by checking retailers with online sites like The Bay, Walmart Canada, and Babies "R" Us. And don't forget that eBay and craigslist are often great, inexpensive sources for slightly used items that the seller's baby has outgrown. (We can't emphasize this enough: There is no shame in buying used—especially when it comes to kids' stuff, since they tend to outgrow toys and clothes long before they're worn out.)

Don't be discouraged if the prices seem out of reach right now. In the next few chapters, we'll not only show you how to save your money but how to make more, too. We don't just want you to plan your perfect day, but to plan *for* your perfect day so that you can make it happen!

As we mentioned earlier in the chapter, Katie and Nick realized when they did the Perfect Day exercise together that they'd previously underestimated how important it was to each of them to start their own family and to make sure they spent more quality time together, travelling and doing different activities. Both of them also wanted to take more steps to stay in shape by eating a healthier diet and by taking more classes in sports or activities that interested them. So they sat down together and came up with three goals they wanted to achieve over the next year: have a baby, take a three-week vacation to the Bahamas, improve their eating habits, and be more active. Then they did the necessary research to figure out how much it would cost to achieve them. They were comfortable using money they've already saved up to cover some of the costs—particularly, of having a baby (as they'd been diligently setting money aside for that for several months)—but they also wanted to try and cut their own expenses, or see how they could lower the costs of their goals, to save more money. Together, they were able to save a whopping $8,400. Here's how they did it:

KATIE AND NICK

GOAL #1: HEALTH

Eat fresh, home-cooked meals at least four times per week, work out regularly at the gym, and take up at least one class or sport together each season. Estimated Cost: $415 per month or $4,980 per year.

How *we* came up with the price: We currently spend about $150 a week on frozen, prepackaged, or non-organic groceries. After comparing this to the prices of fresh fruits and vegetables and organic bread and meats, we estimated that it would cost at least another $50 a week to purchase those healthier ingredients. Katie also plans on taking two to three cooking courses a year, at an average of $60 per class, so that's an additional $180 a year (or $15 a month).

In addition to the $50 per month we already pay for two gym memberships, we'd each like to register for at least one extracurricular class or sport each season—from soccer to snowboarding to yoga or carpentry. After researching the costs of taking lessons or classes and purchasing passes (for skiing), we estimate that we'll need about $100 each per month, on top of what we already pay for our gym memberships, for a total of $200 between us.

How *we'll* get it: Since we're planning on participating in more activities outside the home, we decided to switch to basic cable for just $60 per month, from the $150 we were paying for a bigger package, which will save us $1,080 per year. And we are going to sell our DVR, which should bring in another $200. Katie also reached out to a local yoga studio where she wants to take classes and offered to provide some marketing and PR services in exchange for free passes. These savings add up to $2,030—or about $169 per month— almost half the cost of activities. We'll draw the remaining $246 per month from savings we've already built up for short-term goals.

GOAL #2: FAMILY

We want to have a baby in the next year, and have enough savings to cover related expenses, including child care, as well as regular trips to see extended family. Estimated Cost: $1,866 per month (including child care) or up to $20,000 the first year.

How *we* came up with the price: After checking local and online baby stores, we've estimated the cost to furnish the baby's room and purchase clothes, toys, carriers, a stroller, and other accessories, at as much as $10,000 for the first year. Katie plans to stay home with the baby for six months, then we've estimated we'll need to spend about $1,000 per month on child care. (That's based on talking to friends who are parents as well as looking at local child care services.) By averaging the costs of airline tickets to see our families, we've estimated that we'll need to save about $4,000 the first year to be able to visit them as often as we'd like in the year after our baby is born.

How *we'll* get it: We are currently saving one of our salaries and using the other's to cover expenses. The money we save will primarily be used to cover the expenses related to starting a family. We've agreed that Katie will go back to work within six months of having a child. Since she is self-employed and has hardly any government assistance for maternity leave, she decided to return to work to be able to cover ongoing child care costs and afford to have additional income to visit family and friends out of town.

GOAL #3: Travel
We want to take a three-week vacation to the Bahamas over the holidays. Estimated Cost: $7,300.

How *we* came up with the price: Round-trip flights between Vancouver and Nassau can cost as much as $1,800 per person in peak season. We also discovered that the costs of accommodations can range from $150 to $500 per night.

How *we'll* get it: Katie has been saving up frequent flyer points and has enough now to cover one round-trip ticket to the Bahamas. That means we may need to fly separately, but we feel like that is a small price to pay for an estimated $1,800 in savings. We plan on booking the second flight early through a discount website like www.hotwire.com. We found that by taking two connecting flights, and travelling for an additional eight hours, we could save another $700 on Nick's flight—well worth the time! We are also planning on renting out our condo over the holiday season for at least part of the time we're away. We expect this will earn us an additional $800. And instead of staying in a hotel while we are in the Bahamas, we connected with some local expats who plan to head out of town for the holiday season, and they are letting us stay in their home for free—as long as we keep it clean and water the plants. Since we'll be staying in a home, we plan to eat more of our meals in, which we estimated should save us about $900 over those three weeks. Those savings, plus the extra earnings we plan to get from renting out our condo for a week, should cover about $6,200 of the original cost estimate we came up with. We'll use our savings to pay for the rest.

There are a lot of ways you can both cut the cost of your goals and save more money to put towards them. In the next few chapters, we'll help you design a plan that's just right for you. Just remember: Setting money aside for those larger goals doesn't mean you can't have fun in the meantime. It's just a matter of prioritizing.

Once you commit yourself to setting a certain amount of money aside for the longer-term goals that really matter to you, a funny thing happens: You'll find that short-term spending (that is, spending that yields little return in the long run) becomes less appealing. You'll both start looking at how you spend money in a whole new way, asking yourself—and maybe each other—if each of the purchases you make is really *worth* your hard-earned money. Trust us. It will get easier to say no to things you don't really need, like a new flat-screen TV or another $100 pair of jeans, if you know that saying yes would mean waiting that much longer to reach your bigger goals. This does not mean that you can't splurge occasionally. It's just a matter of where you *want* to put your money and when.

Cut Costs Without Cutting Out the Fun

If you're gourmands who love to sample the prix fixe menus at the top-rated restaurants in your area, then do it! Just make sure that dinners like that are an occasional treat and don't get in the way of your bigger goals. That's what Sandra and her boyfriend, Jason, have done. They agreed to eat at home most nights so they could save up and splurge on an occasional four-star meal to satisfy their foodie cravings. But if you both have dreamed about something bigger—say, taking a week-long cooking course in Tuscany—then you might decide to skip even the occasional five-course meal and simply sample an appetizer and a drink at the restaurant's bar. That way you can put the money you save towards your bigger goal (the tuition and trip to Tuscany), and make it happen sooner.

If you're huge hockey fans, why not go in on a pair of season tickets with several friends so you can each go to a few games that season but spend a lot less? On those nights when you aren't watching the game live, you could organize a Hockey Night In, and invite other fans over to share a pizza or potluck dinner and watch the game together on TV. Imagine what you could do with the money you save? You might be able to buy a pair of playoff tickets, if that's on your list of goals. Or you could use some of the savings to take hockey lessons, if that's a personal goal, or to buy a jersey or other memorabilia autographed by one of your favourite players. The idea here is to start putting more of your money towards those bigger goals, rather than spending it all on the smaller stuff.

Think about some of the short-term and long-term goals you came up with together. Now, take a good look at the worksheet that shows where your money has been going in a typical month. Do you see any categories—like entertainment, cable TV, or clothes shopping—where you think you could spend less money? Are you both spending your money in ways that will bring you closer to your perfect day or that will keep you stuck in your present circumstances? Are there places where you question the value you're getting for your money? Are there any expenses that don't seem worth your money once you examine them more closely? As you look at where your money has been going each month, you may find some obvious ways that you can redirect some of it to bring you closer to your goals. As you cut out the spending that doesn't give you much in return and seek out cheaper alternatives to other expenses, you might be surprised at how much extra money you find.

Found Money

After she stepped back and analyzed where her money had been going, Andrea made a list of those things she could live without—or with less of—without feeling deprived (which is important!). The list included: her premium cable, daily Starbucks runs, car washes, clothes shopping, and the dinners and drinks out with friends several nights a week. Next, she started shopping around and brainstorming to come up with less expensive alternatives. After doing some research, she decided to downsize her cable to the basic package and change providers so she'd get a better deal. The savings: $500 a year. She didn't want to cut out her Starbucks trips altogether, so she decided she could cut them in half and still save as much as $75 a month. Andrea was okay with cutting down on expensive dinners, but she didn't want to spend less time with her friends, so they started hosting nights *in* instead. The $6 Girls Night was born. Each Smart Cookie would bring $6 and the combined $30 would cover a bottle (or two) of wine and some takeout or snacks. She also stopped taking her car to the car wash and drove it to her parents' place on the weekend instead, and used their hose and cleaning supplies to wash it herself—plus it gave her a chance to spend time with her family. Finally, she made note of a few boutiques where she consistently overspent and avoided them—or brought along one of us to talk her out of any impulse purchases. By cutting back a little in each area, Andrea was able to save hundreds of dollars each month in "found money" without noticing much of a difference in her lifestyle at all. Of course, she came up with these when she was single. We bet you can come up with even more ideas as a couple.

Claire and Ryan are avid readers who regularly visited bookstores and bought at least a few new titles each month. They decided to start doing their browsing at the library instead, and each got cards. They still shop occasionally at second-hand bookstores. But by checking most of the books they read out at the library instead of buying them, they've saved nearly $40 a month. The Toronto couple also realized they were spending a lot more than they'd anticipated on clothes and toys for their baby girl. So Claire set up a swap with other moms in her area. Those with babies who were a little older were happy to give Claire and Ryan the toys, books, and clothes their kids had grown out of already. In return, Claire brought in clothes from her own closet that she was willing to give away, and also offered to swap some of the toys that didn't seem to pique her daughter's interest. (Different babies have different tastes, so what doesn't interest one may appeal to another.) Claire also decided to forgo a gym membership and work out with other new moms instead. They meet daily, bringing their babies along in strollers, and walk or jog around the neighbourhood. Not only has that saved Claire an estimated $350 a year in gym membership fees, but she now gets to socialize and strengthen her friendships with other moms in the neighbourhood. She and Ryan also started shopping around more to see if they could cut the costs of any of their other recurring expenses, and discovered that if they filled their prescriptions at a large warehouse retailer, which didn't require a membership, instead of the drugstore near their home, they could save about $8 in dispensing fees for every prescription! The changes they made netted them more than $1,000 in found money in a year.

In Chapter One, we mentioned some of the ways Sandra and Jason had cut their expenses to save money for their Hawaiian vacation. By eating out once a week, instead of three times, they saved nearly $300 a month. By saving their Starbucks trips for the weekends, they saved $160 a month. Just by finding a cheaper gas station, and making sure they always fill up there, they saved $35 a month. And by opting for a no-frills car wash, instead of visiting the high-end car wash, they saved another $10 a month (and their car looks just as good). By parking in a free lot a little farther from the hockey arena when they go to Rockies games (her boyfriend gets free tickets through work), they've saved $45 a month. They like to go to the movies at least three times a month, and didn't want to cut back. But by bringing their own snacks to the movies, instead of hitting the snack bar, they were able to save another $45 a month. Total found money: nearly $600 a month!

Together, see if you and your partner can think of at least five ways that you can spend less on expenses, or find cheaper alternatives, without giving up anything you enjoy. Be creative about it. Then tally up how much "found money" you will have just by making those changes. How much faster do you think you'll be able to reach those goals you wrote down earlier if you put that extra savings towards them? Think about that any time you're tempted to overspend.

The Rather Factor

When you're looking at where your money is now going and trying to figure out where you can cut your expenses without cutting into your lifestyle, it can help to use what we call the Rather Factor. This may be a familiar term to those who read our first book. It's a concept we came up with during one of our discussions about the social pressures and obligations that made it challenging to stick with our spending plans (which we'll help you create in the next chapter). Robyn was recounting how she'd shelled out close to $100 recently on an expensive birthday dinner for a friend of a friend. She sighed and added that she would much *rather* have put that money towards the trip she planned to take to Paris. And the Rather Factor was born.

Each of us realized that we'd been spending way too much money out of a sense of obligation, guilt, social pressure, or just out of habit, instead of spending money in ways that would bring us real satisfaction and fulfillment. Once we started paying attention, we were able to re-allocate our spending and direct it towards the people and purchases that meant the most to us. And we each made a point of cutting back on the obligations or mindless purchases that left us feeling frustrated at the amount of money we'd spent.

We're not suggesting that you need to turn down every social invitation that's not from a close friend or family member, or bail on any work function that's not required. But, as a couple, you may decide that in some cases, only one of you needs to attend an event—especially if you have children (then you have to add in the cost of getting a babysitter, too). Or that it makes more sense to just send a gift—say, in the case of an out-of-town wedding of a colleague whom neither of you know well, for example, which would require you to pay for airfares and accommodations—times two. Instead, you can use the money you save for the vacation you'd *rather* take together instead. Or rather than buying a $30 bottle of wine for your party host, why not pick up a small bouquet of flowers. They'll last longer and they'll be a nice reminder the day after the party of your thoughtfulness. Rather than dropping a lot of money on an expensive after-work meal with colleagues, join them for drinks and then eat dinner at home with your partner. (We'll share many more tips on cutting costs without cutting into your social life later in the book, too.)

Fill in the Blanks

Once you've identified a few areas where you can trim your spending, fill in the blanks below. Then share them with your partner. By making it clear what your priorities are, you can help each other avoid spending money out of guilt or habit.

I'd rather have enough money to _____
than spend money on _____.

You can write out as many examples as you want. It's a good idea to also write these out on a slip of paper and then tape that to the back of your primary credit card. That way, it will be there when you're tempted to use the card. It's amazing how much money you can redirect towards your goals just by keeping in mind what you'd rather spend your money on.

Sticking to a spending plan isn't about telling your friends, or yourselves, 'We can't afford *[fill in the blank].*" It's about making a conscious choice about how you and your significant other want to spend your hard-earned money. Don't worry that you're going to miss out on invitations to dinner or to vacation with friends who assume you two won't be interested because you're "on a budget." The fact is, you can still get vacation rentals with friends or splurge on an expensive dinner. It's *your* choice. You can cut back wherever you want, so that you have the money to do those things that are truly important to you. It is just a matter of prioritizing how you spend your money. It's not about being cheap; it's about being in control of your spending.

Rather than thinking about what you aren't buying now, focus on what the money you're saving will bring you later. The satisfaction you'll both get from watching your savings grow should far outweigh any temporary high you'd get from a short-term splurge—and so will the realization that you are firmly in control of your money now and that much closer to living your perfect day. In the next chapter, we'll help you come up with a plan that's customized to fit your needs.

Smart Cookie Summary

Discussion Questions:

1. What do you want your life to look like five years from now?
2. What in your life now brings you the most joy? The least?
3. What activities would you like to be doing more of, or less of, now?

Smart Steps:

1. Describe in detail what your perfect day would include.
2. Name five activities you would be doing on your perfect day.
3. Name five things you would have on your perfect day, which you don't have now.
4. Together, come up with three to five priorities, based on your descriptions of your perfect days.
5. Create a vision board—or some sort of visual reminder of your goals—using photos, cut-out words, and symbolic images that illustrate the life you want.

chapter 4

Do the Math

How Does Your Relationship Add Up?

You may not know exactly how much your partner makes, or how much debt he (or she) has. But do you know what *you* are earning after taxes each month? Without peeking at your statement, could you tell us how much credit card debt you have or how much monthly interest you're paying?

Before you can figure out how you are going to divvy up the expenses and save enough to have the things you want, you need to know those numbers. You have to have a handle on your own finances. And so does he (or she). You've each got to know what you're making, saving, spending, and sending to your creditors each month, before you can adjust the figures to achieve your financial goals together. That means making an honest assessment of your current situation—not what you think or hope it could be, but what it actually is. It also means being willing to share those details with your significant other. That is a critical step towards building your future together. But the first step is to get a handle on those numbers yourself. Take a moment to find your most recent paycheque and encourage your partner to do the same. Next, double the amount on the cheque so you know about how much you are making each month. Do you think it's enough to cover all of your current expenses and still allow you each to set aside money towards the bigger goals you've got?

If you're like most people, you probably couldn't answer *any* of the questions we asked above without checking your statements. And it might take hours, or even days, for you both to dig up all of the documents you need to compile the necessary information. But trust us, it's an exercise worth doing. After all, how can you make a plan to manage your expenses together, much less plan for your future, if you have no idea how much you make or spend first?

By the end of this chapter, you'll know the answer. And it may surprise you. Are you ready to get started?

Know Your Numbers

For this exercise, you'll both want to gather your pay stubs, and bank and loan statements, plus any utility, cellphone, and credit card bills from the last three months (or as far back as you can within that period). It's also helpful to print out a record of your debit card purchases and collect any receipts you have kept from cash purchases. These will help you put together an accurate portrait

smart **SC** bite

You may want to purchase an inexpensive notebook to do this and other exercises from the book and to write down any related notes. When you're not using it, stash it someplace that's private but accessible to each of you. It's helpful to designate a specific drawer or a folder in a file cabinet, where you can also store important money-related documents (like tax forms and loan agreements). Putting all your financial information in one place that's convenient to both of you will make it easier to keep track of your finances and to monitor the progress you're making towards your goals.

of how much money is coming in and going out—and where it's going. We recommend scheduling a time with your partner to do this exercise together, giving yourselves a few days to gather all the information you need first. If you haven't yet had that initial conversation about money, this is a great way to get started. Just remember the tips we outlined at the end of the last chapter.

Once you've each gathered your pay stubs, statements, and receipts, use them to answer the questions below:

- **How much do you earn per month?** This is your average net income (after taxes) for one month. If you typically receive commissions, bonuses, or contract work as well, take the average of what you earned each month over the last three months.

- **How much do you owe per month?** This is the combined total of the minimum payments you each owe to your creditors—whether it's a credit card balance, school or car loan, or a mortgage—plus the average amount you pay per month on bills like rent, maintenance, taxes, electricity, cable, Internet, and hydro.

- **How much are you able to save per month on average?** This is the amount you put into a savings or money market account each month.

- **How much do you invest per month?** This is the amount you put in your retirement accounts, as well as any money you invest in certificates of desposit (CDs), mutual or index funds, or individual stocks or bonds.

- **How much is left?** This is roughly the amount you have to spend on everything else each month—from haircuts to groceries, gym memberships to eating out.

You can photocopy the worksheets on pages 72 to 75 to help you both add up your numbers. Or download them from our website (www.smartcookies.com). Either add up your incomes, expenses, and obligations together; or, if you prefer, do the exercise separately, based on your individual earnings and expenses, and then compare notes.

WORKSHEET

	Month 1	Month 2	Month 3	Monthly Average (Monthly Totals/3)
MONEY I EARN				
Wages				
Extra Earnings				
Income Totals				
MONEY I SPEND				
Utility Bills				
Maintenance				
Cable/Internet				
Cellular Telephone				
Home Telephone				

MONEY I SPEND (continued)	Month 1	Month 2	Month 3	Monthly Average (Monthly Totals/3)
Water Bill				
Home Repairs/Decor				
Groceries				
Meals Out				
Gas				
Car Insurance				
Public Transportation				
Parking				
Gym Membership				
Health Insurance				
Life Insurance				

MONEY I SPEND (continued)

	Month 1	Month 2	Month 3	Monthly Average (Monthly Totals/3)
Home Insurance				
Clothing				
Entertainment				
Other				
Other				
MONEY I SPEND TOTALS				

MONEY I SAVE

	Month 1	Month 2	Month 3	Monthly Average (Monthly Totals/3)
Savings Account				
Investments				
MONEY I SAVE TOTALS				

MONEY I OWE	Month 1	Month 2	Month 3	Monthly Average (Monthly Totals/3)
Credit Cards (or Credit Line)				
Car Loan				
Student Loans				
Mortgage/Rent				
MONEY I OWE TOTALS				
Total Earnings				
TOTAL EXPENSES				
Cash Short/Extra				

If you look closely at your financial documents, you may immediately discover some painless ways to start saving more money. When Robyn examined her bank statements, she realized she was paying as much as $50 a month on bank fees, mostly for having too many debit card withdrawals. She cut those back to avoid the charges and was able to save $600 in one year. Andrea had also been paying fees for too many debit transactions without even realizing it. When she read through her statements, she learned her bank was treating her online bill payments like debit transactions, often pushing her over her monthly limit. She did some research and ended up moving her account to a bank that allowed her to make as many transactions per month as she wanted for free. By doing so, she saved more than $360 a year in fees.

This exercise may also give you ideas on ways to make more money. If you've got a savings or money market account, for example, check to see how much interest you earned this month. Banks often reset rates so even if you signed up for an account that yielded 2.5 percent or more at the time, that number may have gone down. If your partner is getting a better interest rate on his (or her) money market account, you might want to change banks, at least, even if you're not ready to merge accounts just yet. It may also benefit you both to look at how much you're earning on your investments. By comparing notes, you might find new ways to increase the return you're each getting on your own investments.

Going over your expenses can also reveal some easy ways to cut your costs. You might discover that by switching to your partner's cheaper cellphone plan you could immediately lower your monthly bill. Or he (or she) might notice that you're paying a much lower interest rate on your credit card balance and transfer the balance to your credit card company to match your rate (assuming they have a good credit score).

Once you've filled in all of the blanks on the worksheets, take a look at how your numbers add up. Do you think the money you both have left can cover all your other expenses? Are you each saving and investing enough? Let's find out.

Show Me the Money

Now that you have calculated how much you earn, owe, save, and invest, it's time to figure out exactly where the rest of your money is going.

To do this, you'll want to pull out those recent bank statements that show debit purchases you've made over the past three months, plus any receipts you've kept. Use those to come up with an estimate of what you've been spending each month on everything outside of your obligations (like debt payments, rent, or utility bills). Initially, this will probably be more of a guess than a calculation. You can compare the first number you come up with to the actual tally you add up once you start keeping track of all your daily purchases. But right now, you just want to get an idea of how much you're spending on non-essential stuff.

When we first did this exercise, most of us realized that we were spending much more than we'd thought on discretionary expenses and, in some cases, more than we even had in the bank. (That might explain the credit card debt.) Just seeing the actual numbers in front of us motivated us all to change our spending habits so that we could stop adding to any credit card debt and start paying off that debt instead and saving more money.

In the coming chapters, we'll help you determine how much you need to adjust your spending to make sure you're saving enough money each month and show you how to come up with a new spending plan that reflects both your priorities and future goals. Don't be discouraged if it feels like you can barely cover your current expenses. We'll also share some simple tips on how to save on everyday purchases as well as big-ticket items, so that you have extra money to put towards your goals. First, you need to get a clear idea of where your money is going now.

Where Does Your Dough Go?

A simple way to answer this question is to keep a daily log: Write down how much you spend on each purchase and what you buy. Either write descriptions of exactly what you bought or use categories like groceries, gas, meals out, clothes, dry cleaning, or toiletries. Just be sure to include every purchase you make outside of your monthly bills and debt, loan, and credit card payments. You can use the same notebook you've used to do the exercise above. And save your receipts, or keep a mental tally, and then write down your totals at the end of the day. (Using the notebook will give you the space to record notes about your purchases, too.) Or you can just write it in your day planner or type it into a Word or Excel document. Use whatever method is most convenient for you.

After just a few days, you should already be getting an idea of how your typical daily expenses add up, but we recommend that you continue writing down what you spend for at least a month to make sure you have an accurate estimate on which to base the spending plan we're going to help you create later in this book. You might even find you actually enjoy keeping track of your spending and continue doing it. (Some of us still do, years after we started.)

Keeping a log of your everyday spending also makes it simpler to divide expenses with your partner if you don't have a joint bank account. It's less of a hassle than you might think to track what you spend, especially once you get into the habit. Once you've kept track of your purchases for at least a few weeks, you can use the worksheet on page 72 to fill in the blanks. Or download it from www.smartcookies.com. This time, the numbers you fill in should be much more accurate.

Why We Buy

Knowing what you're spending your money on is essential, but it's also important to understand why you're spending it in those ways. Try jotting down your thoughts over the next few weeks before and after you spend money or pull out your credit card. When you have time, take a moment before you make a purchase to write down how you're feeling—or, at least, make a note of it in your mind.

If you've become accustomed to running out for a latte most weekday afternoons, pay attention to what you're feeling just before you make your coffee run. Are you bored? Anxious? Or just feeling lethargic? Ask yourself: What would happen if I skipped the coffee drink today? What if I just went for a walk instead? If you find yourself wandering into a store where you know you'll be tempted to make an impulse purchase, ask: Why am I here? What triggered my decision to come here? Is this something I really need? If I thought about it overnight, would I come back?

Before you order that $12-plus-tip takeout meal, ask yourself if you really want that meal or if you're just picking up the phone out of habit or because you're feeling tired after a long day at work. If so, maybe a small snack (think fruit or yogourt) and a shower will give you the boost you need to make a sandwich or stir-fry some vegetables. Or, if you don't feel like making a meal, why not get a $6 deli sandwich instead of takeout? Or ask your partner if they'd be up for cooking tonight?

Stopping for a minute to think about your purchase before you buy it can actually keep you from spending money impulsively or for the wrong reasons: Because you're bored or unhappy, for example, or just out of habit. It should also get you thinking about what you're getting out of some of the purchases you make, and whether you can get the same amount of satisfaction (or more) for less money. Going on a walk to get some fresh air with a friend from work might have the same effect on your mood and energy level as running out to buy a $4 coffee drink, and for a lot less money. Calling a friend and chatting will probably make you feel better in the long run than splurging on another little black dress you really don't need. A $6 turkey sandwich—or, better yet, a meal cooked by your partner or husband—can satisfy you just as much as takeout and cost a lot less. And it's probably better for you (not to mention you don't have to tip!).

It's also helpful to think about how you feel *after* you make a purchase. When you buy something that's not essential, ask yourself: On a scale of one to ten, how happy am I with the purchase I just made? Do this often enough and you might see some areas right away where you can trim your expenses and find ways to redirect your spending so that it brings you more fulfillment.

Both men's and women's spending habits can be influenced by moods and impulses. So your significant other might want to try the same exercise, too. When you're out shopping together and he picks up an item that you're pretty sure he doesn't need, you might ask him if it's something he feels he really needs or wants. Or encourage him to put it down and walk around the store a little first to think it over. If he still wants it, you can go back. But we've found that more often than not, he won't end up going back for it.

Be a Conscious Consumer

By paying more attention to your purchases, you'll also get a much better idea of how much buying you've been doing unconsciously and become much more attuned to how you are spending your money now. The five of us actually found that the awareness alone was often enough to keep us from making an unnecessary purchase, and the same held true for the men in our lives. Why? One big reason so many of us get into trouble is that we spend mindlessly. We often don't stop to think about whether we're getting actual enjoyment out of the purchases we make or whether there's a cheaper alternative that would make us just as happy.

After they started keeping track of their spending, Katie and her husband were shocked to discover how much it cost for them to eat out during the workweek. Nick calculated that he spent more than $40 a week on weekday lunches, which he mostly bought out of convenience. And Katie, who had started a PR firm, realized she was spending nearly $100 a week on business meetings she'd arranged with current or potential clients in restaurants because she didn't have an office yet. Nick started packing a lunch two days a week and Katie began meeting clients in their own boardrooms or offices. Just by making those small changes, they were able to save more than $200 a month. That's $2,400 a year!

Stephanie and Eric, the couple we interviewed from San Francisco, found several places where they could cut costs when they went over their purchases. Like Katie and Nick, they were surprised by how much they were spending on meals: They calculated that they were shelling out more than $300 a month alone on takeout dinners and workday lunches. Stephanie also hadn't realized how much her husband Eric, an engineer and huge Mark Knopfler fan, spent on Dire Straits memorabilia, while he was taken aback at how much she sometimes spent on shoes. (She's a doctor and on her feet much of the day, and would spend up to $200 for a pair of comfortable shoes.) They decided to make some immediate changes.

They opted to buy some frozen meals, which they could just heat up if they were too tired to cook, instead of resorting to takeout. And Stephanie, who'd often grab lunch on the run during the week, began making two big pasta dishes a week. They'd eat some of it for dinner, and then bring the leftovers in for lunch. As an additional incentive, they decided that money for weekday lunches would come out of an allowance they'd each get. So would the money that Stephanie spent on shoes, and Eric spent on Dire Straits albums. They agreed to set aside about $160 a month each to cover those and other expenses they weren't comfortable paying for from their joint account. The result: Almost immediately, they were spending less on lunches out and packing them at home more often. Each of them also became much more selective about the shoes or memorabilia they bought. Stephanie was even able to bank much of what she was allocated by bringing in leftovers for lunch and just buying a couple pairs of basic well-made shoes each year, then paying to repair them when they became worn instead of buying a new pair.

Small Changes Add Up to Big Savings

You're bound to come up with plenty of your own ideas for cutting costs. Remember that even small changes count. When you add them all up they can make a big difference in your overall savings. Here is a list of ways we cut down our spending. Take a look at these and then spend some time going through your daily routine and coming up with your own list:

- Make your own coffee, or your own lunch, and you can immediately trim your daily expenses.
- If you need a fancy coffee, order one straight up with a shot of vanilla syrup instead of a vanilla latte and pay half the price.
- If you're eating out at lunch, buy a pre-priced sandwich instead of loading up at the deli bar, where the food is weighed and often much more expensive. Or opt for a $2 bagel with cream cheese or a spread for lunch instead of a $7 sandwich.
- Meet a friend for coffee or brunch instead of dinner, and cut the cost of your meal by at least half.
- Make a big meal on Sunday, as Stephanie does, and freeze or refrigerate the leftovers so you can just heat them up quickly for lunch or dinner during the week.
- If you and your partner or husband want to check out that expensive new restaurant, go ahead, but save a little money by taking a seat at the bar and split a dish or a couple of appetizers. That way you'll still get to experience being there, and you can sample the food so you know whether it's worth paying more for a full meal.
- If you want to get some friends together but don't feel like spending a lot on refreshments, why not organize a potluck where each guest brings a dish or beverage? We regularly have Girls' Nights *In*, where we each contribute about $6 to get a pizza, or some other inexpensive food, and a bottle of wine. You can do the same with your friends—or even just plan some date nights *in*.
- Are you in the mood for a movie night? Pick up a cheap bottle of wine, or pop, and some snacks and rent a romantic DVD or something from iTunes. It's a lot cheaper than shelling out $10 apiece for theatre tickets—not to mention another $5 to $10 on snacks (and if you rent from iTunes there's no fear of late charges!). And you can curl up together on the couch while you watch the movie at home, instead of sitting in a crowd of strangers in uncomfortable seats.
- If it's a cultural experience you're after, check to see if either of your

employers has a relationship with any of the local museums, so you can get a discount. Or check out some of the free events in your area. Cities often sponsor free outdoor movies or concerts in the summer, and theatres sometimes have *pay what you can* nights. Bookstores host free readings by famous authors. Many art galleries are also free to the public (assuming you don't buy the art).

There are a myriad of creative ways to trim your daily spending without feeling deprived (we'll give you several more suggestions in Chapter Five), just by paying a little more attention to what you're buying and how much you're spending for it. This is also an opportunity to start thinking about what you're getting out of each purchase, and whether it's worth the money.

Have you ever bought a pair of shoes because the salesperson convinced you that you looked great in them, only to have them sit in your closet for months gathering dust? Have either of you come home from the grocery store with impulse purchases you barely remember putting in your cart? Or ordered an appetizer because the waiter kept pushing it, even though you weren't that hungry? We often spend money for someone else's benefit—the salesperson who wants to earn more commission, the waiter who tries to upsell us to get a bigger tip, the retailer who places items by the register precisely so shoppers will pick them as they wait in line—and not our own. So much of what we spend money on actually gives us very little return for our investment. And the items that mean the most to us are often not the most expensive ones.

Just think about your five most precious possessions—the things you'd scramble to save if there was a fire in your home. Did that $150 pair of designer jeans make it onto your list? Or the new flat-screen TV or Wii game console? What about the $300 cappuccino maker you splurged on for your anniversary? Our bet is none of them made the cut. You're more likely to think of irreplaceable items like photo albums filled with images of yourselves and friends and family, a yearbook signed by your classmates, or maybe those trinkets you brought back from the first trip you took together. What about the CD you burned for him? Or the poem he wrote for your anniversary?

When we asked ourselves which possessions mean the most to us, we all thought of the photos we have of friends, family, and memories we cherish. Other items that came up during our discussion: a wedding album; a journal a boyfriend made when he was travelling, with pictures and descriptions of all the places he'd visited; a stack of holiday and birthday cards from a boyfriend, close friends, and family; handwritten letters from friends; and a worn-out blanket from childhood that still has enormous sentimental value.

Of course, if we were to put any of those items up for sale on eBay, we probably wouldn't get much money for them. But they're priceless to us, and irreplaceable. If you think of the gifts you've received that have meant the most to you, chances are they'll have more sentimental than monetary value. A price tag isn't always an accurate gauge of how much value an item will have for us. That doesn't mean you shouldn't spend money on quality items that you really want. But it's important to remember that we're usually seeking intangible benefits when we spend our money. And once you recognize your motives, you can often come up with ways of getting the same rewards for less money.

As you start to pay closer attention to where your discretionary money is going now, you'll probably notice that you each spend your money in different ways. Understanding the reasons behind those differences can also help you each spend your money more consciously, and more wisely.

Men Buy, Women Shop

It probably won't surprise you to learn that researchers have found women enjoy shopping more than men and that we tend to shop for emotional reasons, not just practical ones (as men are more apt to do). In a study published in the *Journal of Financial Planning*, researcher Tahira Hira, a professor of consumer economics and personal finance at Iowa State University, found that women are twice as likely as men to shop impulsively and also significantly more likely to celebrate good news by, what else, going shopping. (Nearly a third of women said they did, versus 19 percent of men.)

In another study, researchers at the University of Pennsylvania and the Verde Group, a Toronto consulting firm, found that women also focus more on the *experience* of shopping, while men look at it as a mission—or, more often, as a task—that must be completed. Women pay more attention to the personal interaction they have with sales associates and to the store's atmosphere (not to mention the sales). Men are likely to focus on the proximity of parking, whether the store has the item he wants in stock, and how long the store's checkout line is. In other words, women want to enjoy the process while men just want to get in and out of the store as quickly as possible. If you've ever gone shopping with your boyfriend or husband, you have probably noticed that already. There's a reason why so many stores have comfy "man chairs" near the dressing rooms— some even have entire lounge areas where men can read magazines, watch TV, or even have a drink while their significant others shop. Otherwise, retailers know that the men would be nagging their wives or girlfriends to cut short their shopping trips. Sure, there are some guys out there who actually enjoy shopping. But, generally speaking, women and men view shopping in a very different way: As a pleasurable pastime versus a tedious chore.

So what does that mean in terms of how we spend our money? You might be surprised to hear this, but it doesn't necessarily mean women will spend more. Ha. After all, if we enjoy the process, we're more willing to take the time to shop around and find the best deal. But it does mean that women have to be particularly sensitive to emotional triggers, impulsive urges, or even hormonal changes that can lead to overspending. (A study presented to the British Psychological Society meeting in April 2009 found women are particularly susceptible to spending sprees in the ten days before their periods, when fluctuations in hormones "affect the part of the brain linked to emotions and inhibitory control," according to author Karen Pine, a professor of developmental psychology.)

If you know that you tend to go shopping after you've had a bad day— or during that time of month—enlist the help of your partner. Make plans together to rent a funny movie instead, or make dinner together so you can talk about your day. You're bound to feel better, and you'll also be less likely to overspend.

If you are the type who tosses magazines or other last-minute items you really don't need into your cart as you're waiting in line at the grocery store, make a point to write our a shopping list beforehand and stick to it. Try using cash only and bring only enough you think you'll need to cover the items on your list. When you're looking for new clothes, try to focus on only what you need. You can always come back another day if you're still thinking about that cute little dress you put back on the rack. But chances are you won't. And take advantage of the fact that you're willing to take time to shop. That can also save you money. If you're more willing to shop around for the items you both need and find the best deal, you can help cut costs for groceries, household appliances and furnishings, and even clothes for him. Think about it. If he dreads shopping for most things— except maybe cars, music, and electronics—then he's likely to just buy the item he needs at the nearest store, or the first online site that pops up, even if it means paying a little more. If you're more willing to seek out sales or spend the time comparing prices on different sites, you can save both of you a lot of money.

And yes, men can overspend, too—even if it's not on clothes. In its most recent report, the U.S. Bureau of Labor Statistics found that single men in 2007 spent more than twice as much as single women did on alcoholic beverages, 55 percent more on eating out, and 33 percent more on audio and visual equipment and services. In fact, it found that single men, on average, spent nearly $3,100 more overall than women on their annual expenditures.

So keep in mind that you probably want to spend your money in different ways than your partner, and that you don't necessarily have the same strengths and weaknesses when it comes to spending and saving money. And it's easy to fall into "good" and "bad" money roles in a relationship, telling yourself you're just "bad" with money. But those labels can be really harmful, not to mention untrue. When you go through all your spending notes, you'll usually find that there are improvements you can *both* make, and lessons you can learn from each other.

If you can come up with a plan or strategy that reflects your strengths and weaknesses, you can both save money and direct more of your spending towards the purchases that really matter to you most. To do that, of course, it's good to know what kind of spender you each are. To help you figure that out, we've reprinted the spending type quiz from our last book here. You can each fill out your answers then compare notes.

QUIZ: What Kind of Spender Are You?

To identify what influences your spending, rank each of the statements below from one to five, circling the number that best applies to you. Then tally your score to find out what kind of spender you are.

1 = never; 2 = rarely; 3 = sometimes; 4 = usually; 5 = always.

1. I can go weeks without shopping, then drop $500 in one afternoon.

    1 2 3 4 5

2. If I spend too much during a night out, I'll drastically cut my spending the next day to make up for it.

    1 2 3 4 5

3. I often suffer buyer's remorse after a big purchase and end up returning the item.

    1 2 3 4 5

4. I have actually cancelled plans because I realized I was short on funds from overspending in the days before.

    1 2 3 4 5

5. I'd gladly spend more for a litre of milk at the convenience store if it will save me a longer trip to the grocery store.

    1 2 3 4 5

6. I often use my debit card because I don't feel like going to the ATM for cash.

    1 2 3 4 5

7. I wouldn't pick up takeout food when I can get it delivered.

    1 2 3 4 5

8. If I need something, I'll just run to the nearest store to get it.

    1 2 3 4 5

9.   When I'm depressed, I'll often "treat" myself—to some new clothes or a meal—to boost my mood.

1 2 3 4 5

10. I've gone shopping with friends and been surprised later when I looked at the receipts and realized how much I spent.

1 2 3 4 5

11. If I see something I like, I tend to buy it—no matter what the price tag.

1 2 3 4 5

12. I make a shopping list before I go to the grocery store but end up buying almost as many things that aren't on the list.

1 2 3 4 5

13. If I see the words "sale" or "discount," I buy more.

1 2 3 4 5

14. I'm willing to splurge on an expensive item if it's marked down from the original price.

1 2 3 4 5

15. I often find myself explaining, "But they were on sale!"

1 2 3 4 5

16. I've bought clothes that were on sale even though I wasn't sure I'd ever wear them.

1 2 3 4 5

17. I've put items into the shopping cart at the grocery store and then wondered later why I did.

1 2 3 4 5

18. I never look at the price of the entrees when I order from a restaurant menu.

1 2 3 4 5

19. When I check out at the grocery store, I am often completely surprised by how high the bill is.

1 2 3 4 5

20.   I've spent more than I intended to during a night out and wondered
        where the money went.

        1 2 3 4 5

21.   I don't need to have a lot of clothes, but having designer labels are
        important to me.

        1 2 3 4 5

22.   I would rather use my credit card to buy the real thing than buy a
        cheap knock-off with cash.

        1 2 3 4 5

23.   I'd spend a little more for a designer shirt, even if the label only
        appears on the inside.

        1 2 3 4 5

24.   I often find myself arguing, "But all my friends have got one!"

        1 2 3 4 5

(Remember: 1 = never; 2 = rarely; 3 = sometimes; 4 = usually; 5 = always.)

Look below to see what type of spender you are. (And, yes, it's possible to be
more than one kind.) You don't need to answer "always" to exhibit tendencies
towards a certain type of spending pattern. This assessment is meant to serve
as a guide so that you're more aware of the reasons you may overspend.

**If your total score for questions 1 through 4 was 12 points or higher:
You're a Yo-Yo Spender.** You deprive yourself some days and then overcompensate on others, and hope it will all even out in the end. Too bad it doesn't
work that way. Binging and purging isn't good for your diet or your wallet. And
there's the added risk that if you overcompensate too much, you'll bounce a
cheque, max out your credit card, or get stuck with high overdraft account fees.

**If your total score for questions 5 through 8 was 12 points or higher:
You're a Slacker Spender.** To you, convenience often matters more than cost.
You're more likely to buy your lunch at an overpriced deli near your office than

walk the extra blocks to the less expensive sandwich shop. If the cheaper plane ticket requires a stopover or an early-morning takeoff, you'll gladly pay more to sleep in and take a non-stop flight. In some cases, convenience may be worth the cost. But, often, just a little extra effort could result in some big savings.

If your total score for questions 9 through 12 was 12 points or higher: You're an Impulse Spender. For you, emotional urges trump reason when it comes to spending money. It's for people like you that grocery stores line the shelves of the checkout lanes with candy and toiletries and magazines, betting that you won't be able to resist picking up one last thing while you're waiting to reach the register.

If your total score for questions 13 through 16 was 12 points or higher: You're a "Sale!" Spender. The words "sale" and "discount" and "clearance" make you reach instinctively for your wallet even if it means spending more than you initially intended (hey, you're still getting a bargain, right?). Your instincts are right. The problem is that the discount item may not even be something you need. If you're never going to wear the shirt or eat the jumbo-sized package of breakfast sausages that you bought on sale, then they're not much of a bargain at any price.

If your total score for questions 17 through 20 was 12 points or higher: You're a Zombie Spender, paying little attention to where your money goes. You can come home from the grocery store and wonder why—or when—you picked up some of the items in your bags. You often end up with less money in your wallet than you thought you had, but aren't sure where it went. When you spend money without thinking about it, it's very easy to overspend.

If your total score for questions 21 through 24 was 12 points or higher: You're a Status Spender, and you wouldn't dream of cutting corners with cheap knock-offs. For you, the brand matters more than the price, when it comes to clothes, cars, and everything else. If only your income was as good as your sense of style! Good thing there are sample sales, second-hand stores, sites like craigslist and eBay, and plenty of online discounters selling brand names. Now you just need to take advantage of those less expensive options to satisfy your brand cravings. (We'll give you some help in Chapter Six.)

Use Your Spending Styles to Strategize

Once you've identified your individual spending styles, it will become that much easier to come up with strategies that address your individual tendencies and help make sure that you don't let them get out of hand. (We'll help you create a more specific spending plan together in the next chapter.) Often, you'll find that your styles complement each other, and that you can actually help each other overcome your personal weaknesses when it comes to spending money.

Robyn identified most strongly with being a Yo-Yo and an Impulse Spender: a dangerous, but not unusual, combination. She recalled that when she consciously wanted to save money, she would cut back her spending for several weeks and be able to save an impressive amount of money. But then she would reward herself by booking a trip, for example, during which she'd blow right through all the money she'd saved. Her impulsive nature made it difficult to break her yo-yo patterns. She would stick to her spending plan for weeks and then impulsively book a trip when she started feeling overworked or upset and convinced herself that she *needed* a vacation. Robyn applied the same logic to clothes shopping—waiting two months sometimes to buy something new, and then spending hundreds of dollars in one afternoon at the mall. Her impulse to splurge on herself was especially strong after breakups. After her divorce, she splurged on three extravagant trips in one year including a month-long trip to Thailand and she spent thousands of dollars on new clothes! (This might help explain the line of credit with the five-figure debt she had when she joined the money club.)

Now that Robyn is in another serious relationship, she's much more conscious of her tendencies. Even when her boyfriend splurges on something, she is careful to keep her own spending in check so she doesn't fall into old patterns.

Sandra always thought of herself as being a conscious spender, so she was initially surprised when her responses identified her most as a Zombie Spender. But she realized that when she was entertaining or out with friends, she often paid little attention to how much she spent (especially after a glass or two of wine). As a consequence, she sometimes overspent without being aware of where the money had gone. After taking the quiz, she resolved to become much more conscious about her money when she was out socializing. Now, she and her boyfriend, Jason, each figure out ahead of time about how much money they plan to spend when they go out, whether it's with each other or friends, then put only that amount in their wallets. This way, they're less tempted to overspend. Knowing they'll have to find an ATM, borrow money, or pull out a debit card—not to mention tell the other one that they went over budget—is often enough to keep each of them within their limits. "We're both really good at keeping each other in check about sticking to what we'd planned to spend," says Sandra. "In a couple, you have someone to hold you accountable. So why not take advantage of that?"

Jason scored high as a Status Spender, but he tries to keep that in check by being aware and very selective about what he buys. Instead of shopping for a lot of clothes, for example, he picks a few high-quality items that will last a long time. When they go grocery shopping together, Sandra says he prefers to spend a little more for a good cut of meat or fish, even if it means buying a smaller piece, rather than spending the same amount of money on bigger but lower-quality cuts. He's also happy to stay in and cook several nights in a row so he can save up and splurge on one memorable meal with her at a top-rated restaurant, rather than spending that money on a few nights of forgettable takeout or a couple of meals at a mediocre restaurant.

Like Sandra, Angela scored highest as a Zombie Spender. That was no surprise to either of them. When they lived together as roommates, Angela once went to Ikea with the intention of picking up just a few furnishings. Instead, she spent an afternoon walking up and down the aisles, putting any item that caught her eye into the shopping cart. When she got home, she realized she'd paid so little attention to what she was picking up that she'd bought not one but *three* different covers for her duvet! She's recalled other instances as well when she was forced to return items she'd bought and then realized she didn't need or already had in her closet. Not only was the process a big time and energy drainer, but she wasn't always able to get a refund either, so it was costing her money as well. That might explain why she scored high for impulse spending (picking up items on her way to the register before she'd really thought about whether she truly wanted or needed them) and yo-yo spending: She often suffered buyer's remorse and, if she couldn't return the item for a refund, she effectively punished herself by drastically cutting her spending for the next week or two to compensate. That's no fun! Better to be aware of what you're buying at the time, so you can return unneeded items to the shelf *before* you get to the cash register, saving yourself both money and regrets.

Angela still occasionally struggles with the "spend now, worry later" mentality that used to get her in trouble. But it helps that the man she's dating now is not an Impulse Spender, and that he is aware of her goals and her spending weaknesses. So he does his best to help her stay on track. He enjoys cooking for them, so they can avoid spending a lot of money on dinner out. And they make lists before they go grocery shopping for the ingredients so she won't be tempted to put random or impulse items into their cart. They've also come up with inexpensive outdoor activities that they can enjoy doing together at the local mountains or parks, like hiking or running in warm weather or snowshoeing in the winter—each of which costs less than $10 a day. That way, neither feels pressure to overspend when they get together (not to mention there's not a lot to spend money on when you're on a mountain trail or running in the park).

When Andrea took the quiz, she wasn't surprised to find that she was both a Slacker Spender (she admits she'd sometimes have takeout food delivered from a restaurant across the street from her apartment) and a Yo-Yo Spender, trying to offset a $500 shopping spree one day by cancelling plans the next day to save money. As she thought about her past relationships, she realized that she'd often found herself struggling with her yo-yo tendencies with a former boyfriend who earned more and spent more than she did. She didn't want to seem as if she was being a freeloader, so she felt obliged to pay occasionally when they'd go out and to buy nice (i.e., expensive) gifts for him as well. She'd end up spending more than she could really afford and then restrict her own spending in the days when they weren't hanging out to try and compensate. Now she's vowed to stop trying to keep up with the men she dates. If they want to spend a lot on her they can, but she's sticking to her spending plan. (We'll give you more details on how to create your own in Chapter Six.)

Katie found her splurges were usually tied to being a Sale Spender, though she has Status Spender tendencies, too (with 11 points). She has helped to curb those tendencies in part by sharing a joint credit card with her husband for daily expenses, and reviewing the statements together before they pay off the balance each month. Seeing how much less her husband was charging on the card motivated her to cut back as well, says Katie, and made her think twice about every purchase. And knowing that she and her husband would be reviewing and discussing all their purchases at the end of the month made her much more conscious about how much she spent.

As you look at how you each spend money, and how much you earn, save, and invest, remember that this is also an opportunity to start talking about the improvements you'd like to make in each category. If either or both of you have debt, that's an area to focus on first.

We'll give you specific tips in Chapter Six on how to get rid of your debt as quickly and painlessly as possible, but for the time being, you can set some ground rules now to make sure you don't add to it. Talk about when and whether you can use your credit cards going forward. If you decide that putting an occasional big purchase on a credit card is acceptable (something we discourage), figure out now which types of purchases would be okay and which wouldn't. Would you need to discuss a big-ticket purchase before either of you put it on a credit card? If it's something you'll both be using, would you both be responsible for the payments? And how quickly could you pay it off? Ideally, of course, you'd want to be able to pay if off within a month.

You may also want to establish whether your savings account is untouchable except for emergencies or whether you can dip into it to pay for certain expenses and big-ticket items. Do you want to have individual savings accounts for personal splurges, or put all your money into a joint savings account as an emergency fund or a means to start saving for short-term goals?

You don't have to answer every one of these questions right now, but it's important to start addressing these issues. You want to get them out in the open early on in your relationship because you can't operate on autopilot, or on separate tracks, if you want to be financially successful as a couple. You have to be proactive and work together to establish some financial guidelines and priorities. This way you won't derail or disrupt the plans you have together and avoid having some serious conflicts down the road.

In the next chapter, we'll help you identify some short-term, medium-term, and long-term goals together, which may make it easier for both of you to answer the questions above.

Smart Cookie Summary

Discussion Questions:

1. Where does most of your discretionary money go each month? Why?
2. Can you each think of a purchase you've made and regretted later, or a recent occasion when you spent money out of guilt or obligation?
3. What type of spender are you?
4. What are your three most prized possessions? Why?
5. What would you like to be spending more money on? Less money on?

Smart Steps:

1. Gather your pay stubs, bank and loan statements, and utility, cell-phone, and credit card bills from the last three months, as well as a

record of your debit card purchases and receipts that you've kept. Use them to add up how much you earn, owe, save and invest, and spend each month.

2. Start keeping track of your daily spending and consider how you feel about each of your purchases.

3. After you've kept track of your spending for at least a week, use the worksheet on page 72 to write down where your money is going by category.

4. Take the spending type quiz and discuss ways in which you can help each other fight those overspending tendencies.

5. Write down examples of what you would each like to spend more and less money on, then compare lists and discuss.

chapter 5

Save More Dough

How to Pay for a Trip to Tahiti . . . or a Trip Down the Aisle

It's tempting to assume that being part of a couple means you will have twice as much money coming in and half the expenses—the financial equivalent of getting a huge promotion at work and a 50-percent discount on an apartment. After all, you figure, you're bringing in two paycheques now and you're splitting your bills and expenses, so you should have more spending money left over. And it's tough to resist the urge to adjust your lifestyle accordingly. Purchases you might have put off, or at least thought twice about making when you were each living on your own incomes—a new car, say, or a new couch—suddenly seem more affordable when you look at your combined earnings.

Robyn and her ex-husband found themselves in that position. Robyn's in-laws had generously helped them with the purchase of their home, so that their payments would be much lower. Her husband's parents had the best intentions. But when the couple got married and moved into their new place, the money her in-laws had helped them save led to an inflated sense of what they could actually afford. With two incomes (and even more at one point, when Robyn took on another job) and lower expenses, they adopted an increasingly lavish—and unrealistic—lifestyle. They went on several expensive vacations to faraway places and upgraded their cars instead of keeping those they already had, rather than putting any extra money towards the growing balance they owed on their credit cards or into savings. Had they really assessed their situation, there's little question they would have *rather* spent their money in the reverse order: paying off debt, making sure they had adequate savings, and then planning exotic trips and potential car upgrades. But they'd just focused on one side of the equation—the money they had coming in—without really considering the other. Their combined earnings *were* high and their house payments were relatively low. But in boosting their spending to match their incomes, instead of putting the extra earnings towards their debt or at least into savings, they missed a real opportunity to improve their finances and take a big step towards reaching their long-term goals. So by the time they sold their house, they'd racked up a substantial amount of debt. (Fortunately, they used some of the profit they made from the sale of the house to finally pay off that debt. But depending on the financial climate and the housing market, that might not always be an option. And don't forget, you'll be paying a lot of unnecessary interest in the meantime.)

Sandra and her boyfriend found themselves going down that road, too. Their combined income was well above average, and they knew they could afford to treat each other to lavish gifts and expensive meals out, so they did. They probably wouldn't have spent that kind of money on themselves, but it seemed okay to spend it on each other—at least, for a while. When they decided they really wanted to visit Hawaii together, though, it helped to put things in perspective. They knew they'd each have to set more money aside in order to cover the trip without using their credit cards. As they talked it over, it dawned on them that all this money they were spending on each other now might actually cost them later, if it kept them from saving enough to reach their bigger goals or, worse, put them in debt. So they came up with a spending plan together that would help keep them on track to reach their future goals, something we'll help you do later in this chapter. Though they cut back on the extravagant gift exchanges, they found other ways to treat each other—by cooking a romantic dinner, for example, instead of going out to an expensive restaurant, or by planning fun, inexpensive activities they could enjoy together like hiking or going out to the movies (but bringing their own treats). "Jason and I are both big dreamers and I knew if we were going to make our dreams a reality, and if we even hoped to dig our feet into the sand in Hawaii, we would have to make some changes," says Sandra. "But what amazed us was that neither of us felt like we were depriving ourselves of anything. In fact, we enjoyed coming up with creative ways to spoil each other without spending a ton. And the more excited we got about the trip, the more we wanted to save!"

When you're in a couple, managing your money means finding a balance between the things you want now and those you want in the future. (Trust us: It's absolutely possible to have a fabulous life now and still set aside enough to fund your future goals, too.) But as we keep on saying, it also means finding out *all* the facts about each other's finances, then figuring out how you're going to manage them together. You can't afford to make decisions that are just based on assumptions or on the things you want right now, or you may end up paying for it in the future.

So, as you've probably realized, just because you now have two incomes doesn't mean you have a lot more money to spend. It's possible that one of you might earn a lot less than the other or *owe* a lot more. So you may have less money coming in than you thought, and more obligations than you anticipated. Nor can you base your spending on the assumption that your incomes will only go up, or even that you'll both remain employed—something many couples learned the hard way when the economy went south in 2008.

There's also no guarantee that you'll keep your costs down by sharing them. Sure, the money you can save by moving in together and splitting the rent and utilities can be substantial. But, eventually, you'll want a bigger space—certainly if you want to start a family. You may also want to buy instead of renting, which means coming up with a down payment, closing costs, taxes, and fees on top of the monthly mortgage payment. In the long run, the value of your home should go up, so you'll make some of that money back. And having kids has its own intangible rewards. Still, buying a home or starting a family requires a lot of money upfront, generally a lot more than what you have when you first embark on your life together. Saving enough is easy to do though *if* you don't get caught up in the belief that you can spend more now that you've got more household income. Put that money in an interest-bearing account instead, and you'll be surprised at how quickly it adds up.

It's also possible that one or both of you will actually be in the red—owing more than you have—when you get together. If so, you need to make a priority of paying off any "bad debt" (a credit card balance, car loan, or credit line, for example). Otherwise, you'll end up throwing a lot of your money away on interest payments to creditors that could be going towards your goals instead. Plus, that debt could be dragging your credit score down, which will make it more difficult to get a mortgage or school loan, and may end up costing you more in interest if you do. (The lower your score, the tougher it is to get credit, and the more you'll generally pay for it.) If you have a lot of debt and are wondering how to pay it off, you may want to read the next chapter on getting rid of debt and improving your credit before you fill out the spending plan worksheet in this chapter. But, generally speaking, you want to put as much money as possible towards paying off those high-interest balances as quickly as you can. It's worth cutting your spending, or even putting a little less into your savings temporarily, to pay that obligation off faster. That way you can save hundreds or more in interest payments. Think of it this way: Once you've already got an emergency cushion of savings (enough to cover about six months' worth of expenses), it's hard to justify putting money into an account netting 1 or 2 percent rather than putting it towards a balance on which you are paying 12 to 15 percent. The 1 to 2 percent you make in interest on that money hardly offsets the 12 to 15 percent interest you're paying on your remaining debt.

However much you choose to put towards that debt, just make sure you aren't adding to it. It is rarely too little income that keeps people from reaching their financial goals; it's too much spending. It's the area of your finances over which you have the most control. It doesn't matter if you earn $25,000 a year or $250,000, if you overspend, you're not going to get any closer to living that perfect day. Sure, we're going to show you ways to increase your earnings, and we encourage you to do what you can to make more. But the biggest step you can take right now to reach your goals is to adjust your spending in order to save enough to afford them.

So how do you determine how much you need to modify your spending? The simplest strategy is the workback method. Look at the three goals that you and your partner have decided to make a priority (see Chapter Three) and how much you've estimated it will cost to make them happen. What is your timeline? Six months? A year? Five years? Start from the day you want to achieve your goals and work back to figure out how much you need to be saving each month. So, for example, if you want to buy a house in two years, start with the total amount you'll need to have set aside by the end of two years to make it happen, keeping in mind that housing prices could go up between now and then. Next, divide that by 24 (for 24 months). That's how much you want to start saving each month, making adjustments for other financial milestones or expensive events that could affect your ability to make it happen, like Christmas or a big holiday. If you think you can save more, then you can adjust your timeline. Worried you won't be able to save that much? Then start with a smaller amount and push your target date back, at least temporarily, until you're able to set aside more each month.

Once you've determined how much you need to save on a monthly basis, you can divide what's left to cover debt payments, fixed expenses like rent and utilities, and your retirement contributions. Put the rest towards your discretionary expenses, those over which you have the most control, like how much you spend on eating out or entertainment. The idea is to *start* by allocating money for your goals and your future—in essence, paying yourselves first—and then using what's left to cover your day-to-day spending.

One of the fastest ways to reach your goals as a couple is to try living on the higher income and putting the second income into savings, extra debt payments, and investments. If possible, this is the ideal formula. Not only will you save money a lot faster, but it protects you in the event that one of you loses a job or takes a pay cut. And if you have kids, you've got a lot more flexibility in deciding how much time one or both of you want to take off from work to be with them, since you know you can live on one salary.

Of course, we realize this isn't easy to do—especially if you each felt like you were barely getting by on your own incomes. But it's a formula worth trying to adhere to, if at all possible. If you find you're really struggling to cover your expenses on one salary, you can always dip into the other person's savings. Just remember that the objective is to eventually live on *one* income.

Here's how Katie and Nick are doing it: Nick earns more right now, so they've decided to live off his income. About 88 percent of his paycheque goes straight into a joint chequing account, which they use to pay their bills and cover all their expenses. He also puts about 7 percent into a retirement account, and the remaining 5 percent goes into a brokerage account they use for investments. (They can also tap into that account if they need additional money to cover an unexpected expense, though they have not yet had to do that.)

About 74 percent of Katie's income goes straight into a high-interest savings account. She also puts 12 percent into a retirement account. The remaining 14 percent goes into the brokerage account for investments. Investing is something that both she and Nick enjoy doing. So they've allocated a bit more towards their brokerage account than you might be comfortable doing. The brokerage account is intended to help them earn a good return and reach their goals even faster, but there's always the risk—as we well know—that their stock picks could lose their value, too. They keep most of their savings in a bank account so that they can be certain that the money will be available when they need it, and they know there's no chance that they will lose any of it. By using this formula, they've already been able to save more than $20,000 to use towards their goal of starting a family and are on track for meeting the timelines they set out in the last chapter.

If living on one income seems too difficult—or either of you is uncomfortable with the concept—there are plenty of other formulas you can use. A good one is to live on 70 percent or less of your combined income. Save at least 15 percent, or put some of that towards debt. And invest at least 15 percent.

Megan and Doug have stuck to a similar formula. They decided that half of her income would go into their joint chequing account, which covers all their monthly expenses from the mortgage to groceries, gas, and even entertainment. Doug also puts about 37 percent of his income into the chequing account, partly because another 23 percent of his income is going to pay off

smart Ⓢ bite

TAKE ADVANTAGE OF TFSAs. By now, you've probably heard about the tax-free savings accounts introduced by the government in January 2009. Under Canadian law, if you're 18 or over, you can contribute to these TFSAs. The money can be put into a traditional savings account or used to buy publicly traded securities, bonds, mutual funds, and Guaranteed Investment Certificates (GICs); and any interest or investment income you earn will not be taxed even if you withdraw it.

What you may not realize is that you can also provide money for a spouse's contribution without being subject to attribution rules. So if one of you loses a job, earns a lot less than the other, or takes some time off when you start a family, the other can fund both TFSAs up to the individual limits, for a total of $10,000 (or more) per year. That can result in *big* tax savings for both of you. In 2009, the maximum contribution per person was $5,000. But if either of you can't contribute the maximum, the difference can be carried over and added to the next year's limit.

The indexed amount will be rounded to the nearest $500. For example, assuming that the inflation rate is 2 percent, the TFSA dollar limit would remain at $5,000, for 2010 and 2011, but would increase to $5,500 for 2012.

And don't forget that you can also replace any amount you withdraw without penalty. www.tfsa.gc.ca

remaining debt. Where does the rest of their income go? When they came up with their spending plan, they agreed on a list of personal expenses—like weekday lunches, gym memberships, and cellphone bills—that they would each be responsible for covering. Megan uses about a quarter of her salary to cover her personal expenses and Doug uses 17 percent of his paycheques to pay for his. The remaining income is divided between savings, retirement and investment accounts, and other debt.

To Merge or Not to Merge?

Even if you already share the cost of your expenses, we realize it doesn't mean you necessarily share a bank account. As you start discussing and planning out savings, investments, and spending, or how to pay off any lingering debt, though, the question of whether to open one will inevitably come up (if it hasn't already). Whether you decide to open a joint account or to maintain separate ones is up to you. We don't advocate one arrangement over another. Just make sure you have a set-up that makes you both comfortable, whether that means pooling all your money in joint accounts, keeping separate accounts, or some combination of the two. To help, we've outlined the three options below, along with some pros and cons for each, and questions to ask yourselves before you decide on one.

Mixing the Dough: Joint Accounts

Questions to ask first:
- Are you prepared to talk regularly with each other about money matters?
- Are you willing to take the time to review your bank statements together?
- Do you completely trust your partner to use your joint funds responsibly?

- Are you both on the same page when it comes to how you save and spend your money?
- If your partner has more personal expenses than you do, are you comfortable using funds from your joint account to cover them?
- If your partner brought debt into the relationship, are you okay with using joint funds to pay it off?
- Are you at ease with your partner having access to information about all of the purchases you make on a daily basis?

Pros: Pooling all of your money is a sign that you are totally committed to each other and to a future together, which can be reassuring. It also means you need to have regular conversations about your money, which is essential if you're trying to stay on track to reach your goals. Sharing accounts also adds a layer of accountability. If you know you're going to have to explain a big purchase to your spouse, you might think twice before you actually buy it. It's a good tool to help you keep your spending in check. Merging your money also makes joint expenses easier to handle, since you're only dealing with one account and one chequebook now.

Cons: If one of you has debt or significantly higher personal expenses, you need to make sure the other person is comfortable contributing joint funds towards them. If not, this could be a serious source of strife. You also want to figure out who will be responsible for what early on. If one of you ends up bearing the brunt of managing the money by default, that could lead to resentment about the extra work (and risk leaving the other person in the dark, which we definitely don't recommend). However you divide the responsibilities, both of you need to stay on top of your balances and be aware of where the money is going. This also means having less privacy and independence in deciding how the money you earn is spent.

Sharing the Dough:
Joint and Separate Accounts

Questions to ask first:

- How much income is each of you comfortable contributing to the joint chequing account?
- Should the person with the higher income contribute more? And, if so, how much more?
- Which expenses will come out of the joint chequing account?
- What kinds of expenses will you each be responsible for individually?
- Will you both get allowances from the joint account or will you cover all personal expenses through your individual accounts?
- Does one need to get the other's approval before making any big purchase with money from the joint account?
- What's the most one of you can take from the joint account for a non-essential purchase without getting the other's approval?
- Will you set up a joint savings account, too, for common goals? If so, how much will you each be responsible for contributing?

Pros: This set-up allows each of you some privacy and control over what you do with the money you earn, while still contributing to your common goals and expenses. It's well suited for couples in which one person came to the relationship with credit card or school loan debt and feels strongly about paying off the balance on his or her own or if both of you did and you want to pay off your individual balances before combining all your money. It also works if one of you has higher personal expenses and doesn't feel comfortable asking the other to help cover them. You might decide to each take a set amount from the joint account for personal care, and if you exceed it you have to use your own funds. Not only does that instill a sense of fairness, but it also provides an incentive to keep your own spending in check. (If you know that going above the limit means dipping into your personal savings, you might think twice about booking that massage.) The combined approach also exposes each of you to the other's money-management style, so you can gain a better understanding of the other's approach before you combine everything. Who knows, you might also pick up some good money-management tips.

Cons: The combined joint and separate accounts approach requires more work upfront and can lead to confusion, and even conflict, if you aren't clear on exactly what will and won't be covered out of the joint account. Not only do you need to figure out which expenses come out of the joint account and which don't, but also what kinds of purchases qualify as "joint" and what don't. Also, if there's a big disparity in your take-home salaries, you'll need to discuss how much you're each comfortable contributing to the joint account. (One option: Consider having each of you contribute the same *percentage* of your income to the joint account. That way, there'll be a sense of equality, no matter how much each of you is actually earning at the time.)

Dividing the Dough: Separate Accounts

Questions to ask first:
- . What are the benefits of maintaining separate accounts now?
- Do you plan to open a joint account in the future? Why, or why not?
- Do either of you have debt that you want to pay off yourself?
- Do either of you have personal obligations (e.g., child support) or expenses (hair, gym membership) that you feel you should be responsible for yourself?
- How will you divide joint expenses?
- Who will be responsible for paying the bills? For buying joint purchases?
- Are you keeping your money separate because you don't trust your spouse to use your joint funds responsibly? (If so, this is an issue you need to discuss.)

- Are you keeping your money separate because you're worried that one of you is more committed to the relationship than the other? (Again, if so, you need to address this issue.)

Pros: Having separate accounts gives each of you a great deal of autonomy when it comes to deciding what you do with the money you earn. That may be important to each of you, particularly if you've been successfully managing your money on your own for several years, and enjoy doing so. It can also work well when one person has large obligations—like child support, for instance, or a lot of credit card debt—that he or she isn't comfortable covering from a joint account. It can also work for couples who moved in together before getting married and may have become accustomed to splitting the rent or mortgage and bills while keeping their own accounts. It may seem easier to maintain that system if it's been working well, particularly if one person enjoys being in charge of the bill paying and the other prefers to take a back seat (as long as you're both involved).

Cons: If either of you tends to overspend, then maintaining separate accounts probably won't do much to help you curb it because no one's holding you accountable. Plus, keeping your cash in separate accounts can make paying your shared expenses more of a hassle. Not only do you have to figure out who's in charge of making sure the bills get paid, and who's responsible for what portion, but you have to decide how much each of you should contribute for variable expenses like car repairs or gifts for family members or friends. There's also the question of how you're going to save up for future goals. It's a lot easier when you have a joint savings account and each contribute a set amount, or percentage, each month. Think about vacationing together: How much do you each need to save and who will cover what? It can get tiresome, especially on a vacation, to have to add up every single expense you take care of—from meals out to museum tickets to hotel room charges—and then ask your spouse to pay you back for half (and vice versa). But if you don't keep track, or agree on how much you're each contributing, one person can be left

feeling resentful. That's no fun either. The fact is, when you're maintaining separate accounts, sharing anything beyond fixed expenses can get a little messy.

Arm Yourself with a Plan

Just as you need to come up with the arrangement of accounts that works best
for both of you, you want to create a spending plan that will work for both of
you. Take a look at the worksheet on page 110.

You'll notice that it's similar to the one in which you filled out how much
you're now spending on bills and purchases (page 72). But we're going to use
this one to create a spending plan for both of you that reflects your goals, values, and priorities. (Again, you can either photocopy the worksheet in this book
or download one from www.smartcookies.com.)

Start by writing down how much you want to save each month in order
to reach your goals, how much you want to put towards your debt, if you have
any, and how much you want to put into a retirement account. We'll help you
decide how to invest your money for the best returns later in this book. But,
for now, it's important just to get used to setting aside a specific amount each
month for your future.

Next, write down how much you spend each month on your rent or
mortgage and non-negotiable expenses like water, hydro, and phone (cell
and/or land line). We've got tips on ways to cut some of those bills later in
the chapter, so you might want to use a pencil. Or you can make two copies
of the worksheet. Once you've found ways to trim your expenses, fixed and
variable, you can write out another spending plan to reflect the savings.

You'll also notice a line marked "Fun Money." This is your guilt-free
spending money. Divide it in half and use it to cover day-to-day incidentals
and activities—from a fancy lunch with co-workers to a bagful of candy for
your office drawer—that aren't included as regular expenses or to cover anything above the amount you've allocated for a specific line item (say, clothing).
You can spend it on absolutely anything you want without having to justify it.

SPENDING PLAN

	Month 1 / Est.	Month 1 / Act.	Month 2 / Est.	Month 2 / Act
INCOME				
Wages				
Extra Earnings				
INCOME TOTALS				
EXPENSES				
Utility Bills				
Maintenance				
Cable/Internet				
Cellular Telephone				
Home Telephone				
Water Bill				
Home Repairs/Decor				
Groceries				
Meals Out				
Gas				
Car Insurance				
Public Transportation				
Parking				
Gym Membership				
Health Insurance				
Life Insurance				
Home Insurance				
Misc. Spending				
Clothing				
Entertainment				
Fun Money				
Other				
EXPENSES/SPENDING TOTAL				

SPENDING PLAN (continued)

	Month 1 / Est.	Month 1 / Act.	Month 2 / Est.	Month 2 / Act.
SAVINGS				
Investments				
Savings Account				
SAVINGS TOTAL				
MONEY OWED				
Credit Cards (or Credit Line)				
Car Loan				
Student Loans				
Mortgage/Rent				
MONEY OWED TOTAL				
TOTAL EARNINGS				
TOTAL EXPENSES				
CASH LEFT				

smart $\mathbb{SC}$ bite

SPARE CHANGE. Need some help finding extra money right away? Here's a list of five seemingly small daily purchases that can add up to a lot of money, along with a few alternatives that will help you end the day with extra cash in your pocket:

COFFEE: We're not saying you should go without your daily java, but do the math. There's a reason why personal finance guru David Bach's Latte Factor became a household term. If you both get a daily $3.50 caffeine fix, that adds up to more than $2,500 a year! Just by substituting a specialty drink with a regular $1.50 cup of coffee on weekdays, and saving the lattes for weekends when you can linger over them, you could save more than $1,000 a year.

DRINKS: Even if you only go out one weekend night, and stick with a couple glasses each of reasonably priced wine (say, $8 a glass, including tip), you're still spending at least $1,664 on alcohol a year as a couple—and that's just one night out. (If you live in a major city like Toronto, you can expect to pay even more. A glass of wine in a downtown restaurant can cost $11 or more, not including tip.) Again, we're not advising that you stay at home or stick to water, but you can save a lot by scheduling a date night *in* and buying a bottle of inexpensive wine, for example, or having friends over on the weekend and splitting the cost of refreshments.

BOTTLED WATER: A big bottle can average about $2. That adds up to nearly $1,400 a year, if you're both buying a bottle of water a day. It's really easy to cut that cost—and do your part for the environment—by buying one bottle and then refilling it at the office water cooler (or with your own filtered water). Or springing for a Brita water filter and a couple of Thermoses.

VENDING MACHINE SNACKS: It's midafternoon at the office, and you've got the munchies. But you don't have time to go far for a bite. So you head to the vending machine for a pop or a snack. If both of you do this daily at work, it can add up to more than $500 a year (assuming your snacks are about $1 apiece)—not to mention the extra, often empty, calories. Vending machine snacks aren't so good for your waistline or your wallet. Why not buy some healthy snacks in bulk—think dried apples, baked pita chips, or veggies and a low-fat dip— and pack a sack to bring to work. You can save yourself money *and* unwanted pounds.

WEEKDAY LUNCHES OUT: This was one all our couples cut back on. Even if you're just running out for a sandwich and chips or a drink, you could easily end up spending $7 or more on lunch. Between the two of you, that could add up to more than $3,600 a year. Why not spend about $20 a week on bread, lunch meat, veggies, and condiments instead, and make your own sandwiches. You could save a whopping $2,500 a year!

Use it to treat yourself and a friend to dinner, to indulge in a one-hour massage or tickets to a hockey game, or buy a month's worth of mocha lattes. It's just like having a little reserve fund that you can use for items you might not have included in your spending plan, or to buy yourself a little extra something without feeling any guilt.

We have each allowed ourselves $100 a week in "Fun Money," though you can choose any amount you want. Some of us take that money out of our personal or joint accounts and put it in an envelope. Others use charge cards that must be paid off in full each month (keeping in mind the $400 limit). We can spend it on lunches out, a night at the movies, or to purchase music or movies online—whatever we want. Robyn often saves her fun money up and then buys one expensive item of clothing. Andrea usually uses it for coffee drinks or cocktails with friends during the week. Angela sometimes likes to dip into her fun fund for books or wander the aisles at the drugstore, filling her cart with magazines, lip gloss, nail polish, and any inexpensive item that happens to catch her eye. Whatever you want to use it for, you can. No excuses necessary. We found that having a little extra money set aside to use for whatever we felt like buying helped each of us stick to our spending plans without feeling deprived and allowed us to indulge in the occasional impulse purchase or big night out without getting off track financially. The only rule is that once that money is gone, we have to wait until the next month to refill the envelope.

Now, with the money that's left from your earnings, fill in the remaining blanks for discretionary expenses like clothes, meals out, etc. Don't fret if the numbers look low. We're going to show you how you can stretch each dollar to get the most for your money. You'll hardly notice a difference in your life, but you'll see a difference in your bank balance.

Living Large on Less

Saving money for the future you want doesn't mean you have to feel guilty about every cent you spend on yourself now. Who would want to stick to a plan that entails that much suffering?

The Smart Cookies and our partners are all about preserving the lifestyle we enjoy, just doing it for less. We have managed to find lots of ways to curb our spending without feeling like we are giving up the good things in life. When it comes to deciding what spending strategies work best for you, it's important to come up with some that fit with your lifestyle, not just your goals. We're not asking you to stop going out for dinner altogether, or to swap your digital camera for a disposable one just because it's cheaper. The idea is to figure out what is really important to you, and what's not. The fact is we spend a lot of money on things that don't provide a lot in return. And we often overpay for everyday purchases. (Generally speaking, if you're paying full price, you're probably paying too much.) But with a little creative thinking, it's not hard to find ways to save money without sacrificing our social lives, stylish furnishings, or the small luxuries that brighten our days.

Some cuts should be obvious to you by now: If you haven't watched HBO or TLC in more than six weeks, maybe it's time to switch to standard cable. If you're spending a disproportionate amount of your income on takeout, try trading off cooking nights with each other or, if you're too tired to cook, buy a ready-to-eat meal from the grocery store (they're usually cheaper, and you don't have to pay a tip). There are lots of easy ways to cut back here and there without lowering your standard of living. Here are some more of our personal favourites:

Dates and Socializing

- If you're dying to check out an expensive new restaurant, meet there for a drink and split an appetizer at the bar. You'll get to sample the ambience and the menu for a fraction of the cost. Then you can decide whether it's worth coming back for more.

- When you do go out for dinner, consider splitting an entree and an appetizer, instead of ordering two main dishes. Many appetizers (like crab cakes, mini burgers, or antipastos) can fill you up as much as an entree, but they cost half the price.
- Eat early. Most restaurants and bars have happy hour specials between 5 and 7 p.m. on weekdays, with drinks at half price and a range of menu items for $10 or less. Why not meet after work for a half-price drink and split some items off the bar menu? While you'll need to get your drinks and food orders in before 7, you can take your time finishing them.
- Have a date night *in*. Rather than going out for dinner, pick up a pizza or your favourite takeout, some wine, and a movie (or, better yet, pull out an old romantic DVD from your collection). The idea is to block out distractions and spend some quality time together. You can have as much fun at home as at a restaurant, but you'll wake up with an extra $40 or more in your wallets.
- Instead of defaulting to dinner when you make plans with friends, try meeting for breakfast, lunch, coffee, or even a late weekend brunch (which can always turn into an early dinner). If you eat out, the dinner menu is always the priciest. You're likely to have just as much fun no matter when or where you meet up, so why pay more than you have to?

Travel

- Instead of paying for an entire weekend away, book a swanky hotel in your own city for a night. It'll cost less and you can spend a little more on the room and perks, without feeling guilty. Want the best weekend rates? Find a hotel in the financial district. These are typically booked up during the week with business travellers but offer great discounts on the weekends to fill rooms. (Mention that you're a local and you may get another discount.)
- Combine your business trips with vacations. If one of you has to travel for work, have the other join you for part of the trip, and then stay an

extra couple of days after your work has ended. You'll only be paying for one airfare and you'll spend a lot less than you ordinarily would on the hotel.

- Swap homes with someone who lives in a city you'd like to visit. You can reach out to friends, or friends of friends, to see if they're interested in a swap. Or try one of several websites with listings: www.HomeExchange.com, www.homeforswap.com, www.home-forexchange.com, or www.digsville.com. (Just beware that these sites typically charge an annual membership fee of $45 to $100 to post your home and allow you full access to all the listings and owner contact info.)

- Start your travel-plan research with discount sites like www.orbitz.com, www.kayak.com, www.hotwire.com, www.travelocity.com, www.sidestep.com, or the newest entrant, Microsoft's Bing travel site (www.bing.com/travel/), which was launched in June 2009. You can also submit your own bid through www.priceline.com if you're willing to do so without knowing which hotel will actually accept your bid, if any (you can enter specific criteria though, like a 3-star hotel in a specific neighbourhood of the city you're visiting, for example). Hotels.com is also a great price comparison site, with more than 85,000 hotel listings.

Beauty and Body Maintenance

- Exercise with friends or with each other. Health clubs are expensive. Many cost more than $1,000 a year and often require a commitment of a year or more. Gyms count on the likelihood that most members stop going, at least regularly, after a few weeks or months but are still stuck paying monthly dues until their contract runs out. Before you join a gym, consider organizing a group of friends—or just pairing up with your partner—for daily or weekly walks, runs, hikes, or bike rides instead. This way you can be social and be fit, and working

out with someone else will give you added incentive to stick to your
exercise regime.

- Make the most of municipal facilities. Most cities have free or discounted access to tennis courts, swimming pools, and other sports
facilities. Check to see where you can play for less. Some cities offer
free use of boats or kayaks at city-owned lakes, and even free or discounted rentals of golf clubs and use of the range or course at city-
owned facilities.

- Let your hair down. If you're a woman (or a man with long hair), consider stretching out the time between haircuts. If you normally get
your hair cut once every six weeks, try waiting eight weeks instead
and you can save yourself the cost of at least two haircuts plus tips
each year.

- Shop at the drugstore, not the mall, for skincare products. Some of
the most effective and popular products for men and women can be
found at your local drugstore for a lot less. Oil of Olay's Regenerist, for
example, was ranked as the top antiwrinkle cream by *Consumer Reports*.

Bills

- Card it. For long-distance calls, the most affordable rates can often be
achieved through purchasing phone cards. By using these phone cards
in combination with your cellphone, you can get rid of the costs of a
home phone line, which saves at least $30 a month (or $360 a year)!

- Talk less. If you don't use your cellphone that often, see if there's a
cheaper monthly calling plan that allows fewer minutes. Compare rates,
not just between packages but between service providers.

- Lose the land line. If you use your cellphone a lot, ask yourself if you
really need a land line. If you want both, consider a package deal. Look
for bundles. Some companies offer both phone and Internet service for
one low price. (Check out www.consumercompare.org for a comparison of eight different VoIP services.)

- Cut the cable. Do you really need *all* of those cable channels? You could save a lot of money, and maybe free up some time, by just using basic cable. By giving up cable, Sandra saved both money—$900 a year!—and time. She used the time she once spent sitting in front of the TV to exercise, read, or hang out with her boyfriend, activities which proved to be more fulfilling to her than staring at a screen.
- Go paperless. Read your favourite newspaper and magazines online instead of subscribing.
- Be energy efficient. Turn off the lights when you leave a room. Turn the thermostat down when you're not home. Try a fan before resorting to the air conditioner. Switch to energy-efficient bulbs. Not only will you be helping the environment, but you'll be saving money on your electric bill.

Shopping

- Check for discounted display items. When we are making a major purchase, we always ask the salesperson if the store has any of last year's items on sale or if there's a display or demo model for sale. This works for cars, appliances, mattresses, and almost any big-ticket item. You would be surprised at how much you can save.
- Buy in bulk. Cut down on grocery costs by shopping once a week (where you can load up at a large discount store like Costco) instead of picking up a few items every day at the nearest shop. Always, *always* bring a list when you shop so you don't get sucked into making impulse purchases. And try not to shop when you're hungry and may be tempted by every delicious display.
- Go generic. Most grocery stores offer generic or store brand versions of everything from cocoa to cookies, even diapers and baby wipes. Often the quality is comparable; the generic or store brand versions are just less expensive because they don't spend much on design or marketing. If you pay out of pocket for medicine, you should also

check regularly to see if generic versions of your prescription drugs are available yet. Under law, pharmaceutical companies must allow generic versions of their brand-name drugs to be sold after a certain period of time has elapsed.

- Shop right after major holidays. Buy candy the day after Halloween or Easter and it's typically half price or less. Same goes for holiday decorations and related items. If you have a lot of storage space, plan ahead and you can save a lot by buying a Halloween costume or holiday-related decorations right after the holiday, then setting them aside till the next year.

- Decorate creatively. You can save money by printing out photos you like from the Internet, or photos you've taken, and having them framed instead of buying prints. Or go to a fabric store and buy a piece you like and have it framed. Pick up candles and knick-knacks from discount stores or flea markets to add a personal touch. Try craigslist, the classifieds, or yard sales to find gently used furniture at great discounts. You can always buy a slipcover for the couch if its colour doesn't match your decor—and for a lot less than it'd cost to buy a brand-new couch.

- Join the club. If you regularly shop at a particular store, join its database or see if it offers a frequent shopper card or program. You can join for free and receive coupons and special discounts via email. Some stores also give out coupons worth 20 percent or $5 off your next purchase (respectively) once you've spent a certain amount of money.

- Google it. Before you buy something, type the brand and style into the search engine—an easy way to compare different retailers' prices for the same item. Last summer Sandra wanted two new pairs of high-end jeans. She went to Holt Renfrew and tried on the make and style that she wanted then plugged the info into her online search engine and found exactly what she wanted on eBay. She paid $200 for *three* pairs of jeans that would have cost more than $600 at the mall.

- Prowl the web for promo codes. Once you've filled your shopping cart at an online retailer, open another window and plug the name of the retailer and "coupon" or "promo code" into your favourite search engine. You should be able to find discounts or coupons that you can use when you check out—saving as much as 30 percent or more!

- Sign up for sale updates. Most clothing stores and boutiques now send out regular email alerts to customers on their mailing lists about sales and special events. It takes two minutes to sign up, but the savings can be substantial. Another bonus: You can often plan ahead once you know when your favourite stores' regular sales are, so you can save up your money and then stock up on some of your favourite looks for less.
- Buy some time. If you're planning to shop in the same mall or retail area for a while, put the item you're considering on hold for a few hours. Then walk around a bit before you decide whether to go back to the store and buy it. Once you're out of the environment, and have had some time to think about your purchase, you may decide you can easily live without it.
- Scour second-hand stores. Thrift stores, "vintage" stores, and other second-hand shops are often treasure troves for the savvy shopper. Sure, you have to do some digging, but you can often find designer clothes and accessories at deeply discounted prices. Even better, drop off some of your gently worn clothes, and you may even get an even trade or come home with some extra money as well as extra clothes!

Smart Cookie Summary

Discussion Questions:

1. Do you want to keep separate bank accounts or open a joint account?
2. If you combine your money, what would the joint account cover? What wouldn't be covered?
3. What expenses do you think you could cut without noticing much of a difference in your day-to-day lives?

4. Which of the tips above have you tried to save money? Which would you like to try?

5. How much do you want to set aside for "fun money," if any? How would you spend it?

Smart Steps:

1. Decide together how much you want to save, invest, and put towards any remaining debt each month.

2. Create a spending plan that's built around your savings and investment goals.

3. Open a TFSA for each of you, if you haven't already, and try to maximize your contributions.

4. If you plan to open a joint account, find a bank that offers a no-fee chequing account with a low minimum balance requirement (or none at all). If you're opening a savings account, look on www.bankrate.ca to find the highest-yielding savings accounts available in your area.

5. Over the next week, try out one or more of the suggestions for saving money listed in this chapter, or come up with your own.

chapter 6

Get Back in the Black

How to Deflate Your Debt and Fix Your FICO

If you are in debt, you're certainly not alone. Household debt in Canada reached an all-time high of $1.3 trillion in 2008, or more than $90,000 per household—and that number is expected to grow. In a survey from summer 2009, the Certified General Accountants Association of Canada found that more than four in ten Canadians said the amount of debt they carried was growing. The group says personal debt levels have been increasing 5.5 percent annually on average for the past decade, and may have jumped even more in 2009.

Whether you're trying to pay off a line of credit from your bank, a credit card balance, or a loan you took out to cover the costs of a car or a college education, dealing with debt is tough enough on your own. But when you're part of a couple, it can be even trickier—especially if one of you owes a lot more than the other. If you have been careful to accumulate little or no debt, you may feel resentful about helping to pay off your partner's. On the other hand, if you owe a lot more than your partner, you may feel guilty about having him or her share the burden and be reluctant to combine your finances. Even if you're able to manage the minimum monthly payments just fine on your own, it may seem pointless to plan your future together until that debt is fully paid off. But trust us, it's not. You can *start* saving for your future goals now, even as you pay down your debts. In fact, you should be.

In this chapter, we'll outline six simple steps you can take together to get rid of that debt and boost your credit scores for good, while still setting aside money for your goals.

Step One:

•   **Tally up your totals and set up your strategy.** For this exercise, you'll each need to collect your most recent mortgage, credit card, bank, and car loan statements. Either photocopy the worksheet on pages 126 and 127 or download it from www.smartcookies.com. On the worksheet, list: the total unpaid balance on each debt, the interest you're paying, the annual fee, the minimum monthly payment, how long you've had each loan or credit card balance, and what your credit limit is (if it's a credit card or line of credit). Include debts that you've accrued together and those you may have brought with you into the relationship, or racked up on your own since.

Next you need to figure out how you're going to tackle them together. Are you each responsible for your own debts? Or do you want to pay them off together? Or are you comfortable helping your partner pay down a school loan, but not a credit card balance? Whatever strategy you both decide on, make sure that it's one that makes you both comfortable. (See Chapter Five for options.)

Of all the financial issues you'll deal with as a couple, debt may be one of the most contentious. You may have different ideas about how much debt is too much, what kind of debt is okay, and what's off limits. It is true that some are worse than others, in terms of what you'll pay to borrow it and what you get in return. We'll go through the various types in more depth in the next step. But you each probably have your own ideas about what kind of debt, if any, is acceptable.

Chances are, you each entered the relationship with some debt of your own, too, so if your partner owes a lot more than you do, it's tempting to tell him or her to take care of it themselves. Or, if you owe a lot more, you might feel torn about using joint funds to pay it off, as we mentioned above. There's no right or wrong solution, as long as you can come up with a plan that you can both agree on. But keep in mind that if you attack the debt together, you're likely to pay it off a lot faster and you can potentially save hundreds or thousands of dollars in interest by doing so. No matter who racked up the debt, it might make more sense financially to combine your debts and pay them off together. You may be able to take out a low-interest loan together, for example, to pay off any balances, and then pay off the loan together. That's what Megan and Doug, our Calgary couple, did. When they got married in 2006, Megan had a balance of about $2,000 on her credit card. And Doug had $3,000 in student loan debt. They took out a line of credit to pay off most of their debts, which had a low-interest rate (prime), and then paid that off together.

If you feel strongly about paying off the personal debts individually, though, then do it. You just want to be clear on how you're going to handle each debt you've listed, and where the funds will come from to pay down the balances.

Step Two:

- **Prioritize your payments.** A good rule of thumb is to pay off the "bad" debt first—that which has the highest interest rate, and really serves no purpose (think credit cards). Then you can pay off your "good" debt or neutral debt, which should each carry a lower interest rate, more slowly.

smart **SC** bite

WANT A REALITY CHECK? Use the online calculator at www.bankrate.com or www.fool.com to analyze how long it will take you to repay each debt if you continue to make the same payments. We'll bet it's longer than you figured. But don't worry—we're going to help you speed up your repayment plan.

TALLY UP YOUR TOTALS

	Lender Name	Balance	Interest Rate	Minimum Payment	How Long You've Had It	Credit Limit
Credit Card #1						
Credit Card #2						
Credit Card #3						
Credit Card #4						
Credit Card #5						
Credit Card #6						
Mortgage						
Car Loan						

Student Loans	Line of Credit	Other	Other	Other	Other	Other	Other	Other	Other	Other	Other

The Good: It's best not to owe anything, of course, but not all debt is bad. Sometimes borrowing money now may actually help you make more money in the long run. Taking out a mortgage to buy a home, for example, can more than pay for itself if the home goes up in value—and, over the long term, you can expect it to do so (though probably not in the short term). Yes, the real estate market has fallen dramatically. But that also means there may be good deals for you right now. We'll go into more detail on investing in real estate in Chapter Seven.

While we consider a mortgage a "good" source of debt, that doesn't mean taking out adjustable second mortgages or home equity loans is a good idea. Borrowing against your home with the assumption that interest rates will stay low and your home's value will continue to increase can be a mistake—as many people have found out the hard way in the past few years. There's

smart bite

RISKY BUSINESS. Taking out a loan to start your own business is another type of debt that can pay off in the long run. But starting your own business is always a gamble; more fold than thrive. It's smart to have some start-up money of your own, or at least a cushion to help you through the rough times. If you need to borrow money, it may make sense to turn first for financial help to friends and family who believe in you and your business. They're likely to charge you less interest and allow a longer pay-off period. They can also help absorb some of the risk, if you offer them a piece of the business rather than a specific repayment amount for their loan. Still, make sure to do your homework before you approach *anyone* for start-up money. You should have a solid business plan ready to present to any potential investors.

nothing wrong with tapping into your home equity in certain situations—to pay off high-interest debts, for example (we'll get into that in more detail below). But try to get a low, fixed rate. If you don't have a fixed rate and interest rates climb before you pay off your loan, your monthly payments could, too. If the value of your home doesn't increase very much in the meantime, a real risk in the current housing market, you could actually *lose* money on your investment. Worse, if you're unable to keep up with the payments, you risk losing your house! The foreclosure rate in Canada hasn't been as bad as in the United States, where one in every 398 homes had received a foreclosure filing by May of 2009, but the rate has gone up over the last two years. You don't want to find yourself in that situation.

Getting a government loan to attend college or graduate school may also be worth the investment if you know the degree will help increase your income

Keep in mind that you may be able to avoid getting financing altogether if you start small and choose a business that doesn't have a lot of overhead costs or require a lot of time or money upfront—doing catering or baking, and selling a limited line of goods, for example, instead of opening a full-fledged restaurant. If you can, build your business on the side first, while you keep your full-time job, so you've still got a steady salary. Then, when you've made enough to justify working at your business full-time, you can make the leap. That's what Katie did. She started out doing PR consulting jobs on the side, while she still worked full-time in her corporate job. After picking up extra projects for six months, she'd built up enough of a regular clientele that she was able to leave her job and start her own PR firm.

potential. Robyn literally doubled her income by earning a master's degree in social work. And there's little question that having a master's degree in business administration, or a medical or law degree will help you obtain a high-paying job. Still, it's smart to see if you can finance at least some of the costs of tuition yourself, or if you're eligible for grants or scholarships that don't require repayment. And don't forget that many companies also offer full or partial tuition coverage for employees. Andrea used the $2,000 per year her former employer offered to take four night classes in marketing and other related topics and to pay for textbooks, too. Many employers offer additional assistance for those who pursue an advanced degree while working, if you can demonstrate how the degree will improve your skills and performance at work. Of course, the flip side is that your employer may require you to remain at the company for a set period of time after you've obtained your degree. So be careful if you're pursuing an additional degree to get a better-paying job someplace else.

The Not So Good: Generally speaking, "good" debt has a low-interest rate (under 10 percent). And, ideally, the return you get on whatever you bought with those borrowed funds—whether it was a home, a college degree, or your own business—will more than compensate for any interest you pay for the loan. So what kind of debt is not so good? It's the kind that typically has you paying more than you get in return, like a car loan or a credit card balance.

Financing a car is only good in the sense that you actually have something to show for the money you've borrowed. If you're in a bind, you can sell your car and use the money you make to pay off a good chunk of the amount you borrowed. But you're not likely to make enough to pay off the loan entirely, unless you only relied on financing to cover a small amount of the initial cost of the car. With the exception of collectors' models, a car starts losing its value the minute you drive it off the lot. You are almost guaranteed to lose money on it. Sure, having a car has other benefits. It's convenient to get around, and having a car may even allow you to take a higher-paying job somewhere farther away, in some cases. But a car is also costly to maintain and, depending on the price of gas, it can be costly to drive as well (not to mention parking can be a pain, or pricey, depending on where you live). If you're going to get a car, try to cut your costs where you can. The best advice is to use cash to cover at least some of the cost of the car, so you don't have to finance as much. If you've got good public transportation in your city, you may prefer to put off the purchase altogether. Or consider sharing a car with your boyfriend or spouse. That's what Katie and Nick did. Katie got rid of her car and they share Nick's, a decision that has saved them literally hundreds of dollars. And they used some of their savings to pay off his car loan, which they were able to do in less than two years. If you have an existing car loan, make it a priority to pay that off. And if you do decide to buy a car, always look for a "pre-owned" or used model, which can cost substantially less. Just make sure to have a trusted mechanic take a look at it before you hand your money over.

Still, car loans rarely carry interest rates as high as credit cards. Credit cards—and, to a lesser extent, personal lines of credit—represent the worst kind of debt. That's not only because you're likely to pay higher interest rates than you would for a mortgage or school loan (or even car loan), but because carrying a credit card or credit line balance is an indication that you're over-spending on a regular basis. And a lot of Canadians are, apparently. There are now more than 68 million credit cards circulating in the country, a jump of more than four million from just a couple of years ago, according to the Canadian Bankers Association. And the number of Visa and MasterCard transactions has increased by more than 60 percent in the last eight years. On average, we now carry between two and three credit cards apiece, and those cards get a lot of use. A 2009 report by the Certified General Accountants' Association of Canada found that more than eight out of ten households had outstanding debt on a credit card. By last spring, bank credit card receivables (meaning balances owed) had jumped nearly 9 percent from the year before to $51.5 billion, according to the Bank of Canada.

It's not just credit cards we're using to supplement our incomes. Personal lines of credit reached a record high of $181 billion outstanding last spring, up more than 20 percent from the year before. And personal bank loans were up more than 8 percent from the year before at $48.5 billion.

Having extra credit lets you pretend you can afford a lifestyle that's actually beyond your means—for a little while, anyway—instead of taking action to ensure you *can* actually afford the life you want. It's a double whammy. Not only can you end up paying as much as 25 percent more for your credit card purchase, but you get into the practice of just pulling out plastic and paying for it later rather than saving up money for something you want. With credit cards, you end up spending so much to pay for your past behaviour that it's tough to focus on your future.

Ever wonder how your interest rate payment is calculated each month? Here's how it breaks down: Essentially, your bank looks at what you owe on your card every day. So, let's say you have a balance of $4,000. The bank would multiply that number by your interest rate percentage. If you have a card with a 19-percent annual percentage rate (or APR), for example, you'd multiply 4,000 by .19 to get $760. Then that number is divided by 365 (for the number of days in the year). That means, *each* day you're being charged $2.08. It's as if your credit card company is reaching into your wallet every day and taking out two dollars! Not only that, but the interest adds up between payments. So the interest you're charged each month is actually based on your "average daily balance." That means your balance can go above $4,000 as interest is added, and then you're charged interest on the interest! That's why cutting your interest rate just a little, or paying off your balance even one month sooner, can make a big difference.

We used this example in our first book, but it's worth repeating. If you charge just $2,500 on a credit card with a 12-percent annual interest rate, for example, and send in typical minimum monthly payments (interest plus 1 percent of the balance), it could take you more than 19 years to get rid of your debt and you'll end up paying more than $2,200 in interest alone—almost as much as you borrowed in the first place! We're sure there's a long list of ways you both would rather spend that money.

So, when you're prioritizing your payments, you want the worst offenders at the top of your list: the creditors who are charging you the highest interest rates. You will find that these are usually the credit card companies. We'll show you ways to lower those rates in the next step. But, for now, use your notebook or the back of the worksheet to list your outstanding balances in order of highest interest rate to lowest interest rate. This will help you decide which to pay off first. In some cases, if the interest rates are close but one balance is significantly lower than another, it's worth paying that off first for the satisfaction of having one less monthly payment that you can now use towards another debt. But, as a general rule, it's best to pay off the balance with the highest interest rate first. Paying a high-interest balance off even a few months sooner can save you $100 or more in interest charges. That can go towards paying your next balance off even faster (assuming you have another one).

Step Three:

Get your interest rates down. We urge you both to try and lower the interest you are paying on every credit card balance you have. There's a good chance that you can, especially if you have a good payment history (no late or missed payments, for example) and have held a card for a long period of time (say, five years). But you can be sure that your bank isn't going to offer it to you. You'll have to ask for it, politely but persistently. One effective way is to use balance transfer offers you've received from other banks as leverage. Your card issuer doesn't want to lose your business, if they can help it, and they are often willing to lower your interest rate to keep your money.

Don't give up easily. You will often need to ask to speak with a supervisor in order for your credit card company to authorize a lower rate, or even ask about switching your balance to another card offered by the same bank that has a lower rate but fewer bells and whistles. Make it clear to the supervisor that you don't need points, "rewards," or other features; you just want a plain vanilla card that comes with the lowest interest rate available. (After all, you don't plan to actually use this card anymore for purchases—you just want to pay off the balance.)

If you are unable to convince your bank to match a transfer offer, you might consider transferring the balance. But make sure to check for hidden smart **SC** bite

WHAT YOU SHOULD KNOW ABOUT NEW CREDIT CARD REGULATIONS. In May 2009, U.S. President Barack Obama signed the U.S. Credit Card Accountability Responsibility and Disclosure Act, which imposes several new regulations on credit card companies in the United States. Among the requirements are:

- Card issuers must now give 45-day advance notice of any significant changes in card terms to U.S. cardholders. (In Canada, at the time this book went to press, card companies were required to give 30 days' notice.)
- Credit card companies must now also give U.S. consumers at least 21 days to pay their monthly credit card bills. That may not seem like much, but before this law went into effect the turnaround time could be as short as two weeks.
- By February 2010 some of the most egregious practices will end in the U.S., including: universal default (which allowed credit card issuers to increase their cardholders' interest rates if they were late with a payment to another creditor— whether it was another credit card issuer, utility company, car lender, landlord, or mortgage lender—even if they were never late in paying the credit card issuer); double-cycle billing (a computation method used by some issuers that allows them to apply interest charges to *two* full cycles of card balances, rather than the most recent billing cycle's balances); and certain interest rate increases.
- Promotional or "teaser" rates must now last for at least six months. And interest rates for any cards are not allowed to be increased during the first year on new accounts except in cases in which an introductory period ends, the interest rate

is variable and tied to an index, the cardholder doesn't complete or doesn't comply with the terms of debt repayment plan, or is more than 60 days late with a payment. Card issuers must also start conducting six-month reviews of U.S. accounts in which interest rates have been increased because of market conditions (an excuse many used during the recession), the creditworthiness of the card user, or other factors. If those factors have changed, card issuers are now supposed to reduce the interest rate again.

It's not yet clear whether Canada will adopt all of these measures as well. But a report issued last June by the Standing Senate Committee on Banking, Trade and Commerce called for greater government oversight of credit card companies and recommended that Canada adopt some of the same kinds of measures passed in the U.S. (The committee was to release specific recommendations by the end of 2009.) Finance minister Jim Flaherty also announced some new credit card regulations in May 2009 that are aimed at protecting Canadian consumers. They include a minimum 21-day interest-free grace period on new purchases, a requirement that your credit card statements be easier to understand, and new limits on how banks can contact you about any outstanding balances. Credit card companies will also need to give you advance notice of any rate changes and get your consent before raising your credit limit. They must also clearly disclose just how long it will take you to pay off that balance if you make only minimum payments each month. That reality check alone might provide enough incentive to get you paying more towards your debt each month.

fees and limited time offers. Some banks offer low balance transfer rates for a limited period—say, six months to a year—before the interest on that balance reverts to a higher rate, which can be more than the rate you were paying at the other bank! So be sure that you'll either be able to pay off the entire balance within the limited offer period, or that the interest rate it bumps up to is lower than what you're paying now to justify moving the balance over. Make sure to ask the representative exactly what the rate will be after the set period and whether it is fixed or variable. See if you can get that in writing. And be sure to ask what the lifetime balance offer would be, if there is one available. It may be two or three points higher, but still less than what you're paying now. And if you know you'll need more than six months to pay if off, it may be worth it to secure a lifetime fixed interest rate on the balance you transferred.

Finally, be sure to ask if the transfer fees can be waived or, if not, how much the transfer will cost you. You'll likely be charged a percentage of the amount you're transferring—as much as 4 percent by some banks, as of spring of 2009. So make sure it's worth transferring the money. Do the calculations to be sure that you'll save at least as much with the lower interest rate as it will cost you to transfer the balance. If you have a big balance and don't think you'll be able to pay it off for several months, the fee is usually worth it. But if you owe $2,500 and will pay a $100 fee (4 percent), it might make sense not to transfer the balance and just make sure that paying it off becomes your priority. Of course, if you're paying off your debt together and one of you has a credit card with a really low interest rate, try transferring the balance there.

Katie transferred a $2,500 credit card balance from a card with an 18-percent interest rate to one with a 10-percent interest rate then quickly worked to pay that off before she and Nick got married. Since she was paying less interest, more of her payments were actually going towards the balance she owed, so she was able to pay if off faster and pay a lot less overall.

You may also be able to lower your interest payments by consolidating your debts through a second mortgage or a home equity line of credit. Just remember that these loans require you to put up your home as collateral. So if you can't keep up with the payments—or if your payments are late—you could lose your home. Also be aware that, in addition to interest, you may have to pay "points" on these loans, with one point equal to 1 percent of the amount you borrow. If you take out a loan together with a low-interest rate (preferably fixed) and a manageable monthly payment, then use it to pay off your higher-interest balances, you may be able to save a lot of money in the long run. Just be sure that the calculations work out in your favour over the long run.

Megan and Doug took advantage of this option. So did Claire and Ryan, the Toronto couple with a newborn. They were able to get a low-interest line of credit to pay off the remaining balances on their credit cards, student loans, and car loan. Then they used the money they'd paid towards those balances to pay off the line of credit. Since they were paying 19-percent interest on the credit card balance, the transfer saved them hundreds of dollars. And within a few years, they'd paid off the entire $10,000 line of credit.

Step Four:

Give yourselves guidelines for future borrowing. Even as you're paying off the debt you have, it's important to set some parameters for future borrowing. We don't expect you to cut up every credit card after you pay off the balance and close out any lines of credit you might have. That may help you avoid getting into debt again, but it could also hurt your credit score. If you want to maintain a good score, you want to keep those accounts open and hold on to at least one credit card apiece (see below for more on why). We do recommend that you each take all but one credit card out of your wallets, though, and get in the habit of using your debit card first, so you're not tempted to spend money you don't have. (Or, even better, use cash, which can actually prompt you to spend less.) Keep the credit card with the lowest interest rate, and use it sparingly. When you do, make sure that you pay off the balance as quickly as possible—preferably, as soon as you get your bill. Or you can use a charge card, which requires that you pay the balance in full each month. (Unlike credit cards, charge cards have no pre-set spending limit and no interest charges, but they must be settled in full each month.)

The best idea is not to carry any credit card balance at all, but there may be occasions when you both agree that it's okay to take more than a month to pay off a credit card. Try to agree ahead of time on what types of situations would qualify. You want to discuss not only whether there's a circumstance under which you'd be okay with carrying a balance, even for a few months, but what purchases you're comfortable putting onto a credit card and how much debt you're willing to carry. Will you use a credit card only in emergencies—if you need to book a flight suddenly to visit an ailing relative, for example? Or is it okay to use it to book a vacation or to buy a new couch, if you're committed to paying it off within a few months? You definitely want to avoid getting into a situation where you charge more than you can afford to pay off in a short time period. That means you need to agree beforehand on how much you can each put onto a credit card at one time, and whether you need to get your partner's okay before you charge a purchase over a certain amount.

Some questions to ask:

- Will we each carry our own credit cards or will we get one account with two cards?
- What kinds of purchases can we make with our credit card?
- Are there any circumstances under which we'd be comfortable with carrying a balance?
- Should we set limits on how much we can charge in any given month?
- What's the maximum amount one of us can spend without getting the okay from the other first?

Of course, credit cards aren't the only form of debt you may have. You also need to figure out what other types of debt you're comfortable taking on in the future. What if one of you wants to go back to school or earn an advanced degree or certification? How much student loan debt are you comfortable assuming? And will you pay it off together? What if you need a new car? Are you willing to take out a loan to cover all or part of it rather than using up a lot of your savings? You need to make decisions that are based on your particular needs, goals, and circumstance, though you know where we stand on this one: The smartest move is to buy used and pay cash for it. If you do decide to use financing, try to limit the amount you take on and cover most of the cost yourself.

Even if you vow not to carry any other debtload, there's a good chance that you'll take out a mortgage together at some point, if you haven't already. We'll get into real estate in more detail in the next chapter, but the sooner you talk about it the better. You need to sort out how much debt you're each comfortable taking on to buy a home and how big a monthly mortgage payment you think you can handle. Why not wait and let the bank tell you? Because a lender may approve you for a loan that's much bigger than you can really afford—at least, if you want to reach your other financial goals. Just because a bank is willing to lend a certain amount doesn't mean that you should borrow that much. You need to figure out what amount you can really afford to take on for the long term without stretching yourselves too much financially, stressing yourselves out, or having to put off your other goals.

When Stephanie and Eric, the couple from San Francisco, bought their first home in Chicago, they did some calculations and agreed that they didn't want to take out a loan for more than $250,000. When they applied for a mortgage, the bank said the couple qualified to take out more than $300,000. But they stuck to their guns, since they'd already calculated how much they could take on without straining their budget. "It would have been a lot more difficult if either one of us had wanted to spend the maximum the bank was willing to lend us," says Stephanie. Fortunately, they'd discussed it before they went to the bank and agreed on a range, so there was no conflict. Agreeing on a price and discussing it beforehand also made the house hunt much easier, and more fun. They managed to find the perfect place and put in a successful bid on it after just one weekend trip—something they wouldn't have been able to do had they not agreed on exactly how much they were willing to spend before they started looking. They made a good profit when they sold their house a few years later to move to California. But even if they hadn't made much off the sale, they would have been fine financially. The monthly payments were so manageable that they were able to continue contributing to their savings, too, even with a new baby.

Whether it's credit card debt, a line of credit, a car loan, or a mortgage, you want to be in agreement on how much debt, and what types, you're okay with carrying, and what purchases you're willing to finance.

Step Five:

Fix your FICO. Missing or falling behind on credit card or mortgage payments is not Smart Cookie approved—and it's a pretty obvious slip-up if you're trying to be financially responsible and avoid unnecessary fees and

smart ⊕ bite

GETTING HELP WHEN YOU'RE IN TOO DEEP. If you're in over your head and are falling behind on even your minimum monthly payments, a credit-counselling agency can help to renegotiate your interest rates and minimum payments and set up a payment plan so you can avoid bankruptcy or defaulting on your debt. But beware of agencies that charge big fees or make big promises. In general, you should not expect to pay more than $75 in set-up fees. Before you sign up with a credit-counselling agency, check with the Better Business Bureau in your area to see if any complaints have been lodged against it. And look for accredited, licensed organizations with certified credit counsellors. Try Credit Counselling Canada, a national association of not-for-profit credit-counselling agencies from across Canada (www.creditcounsellingcanada.ca), which can provide the names of member credit-counselling agencies in your area.

interest hikes. But there are several other mistakes you may unwittingly make that can cause long-term damage to your FICO scores—the credit scores most lenders use to determine your credit risk—and to your credit report without you even realizing it. Did you know, for example, that if you close an account after you pay off the balance, it may negatively affect your score? Or that your score may be hurt if one of your creditors lowers you credit limit (something many lenders are doing right now)?

Extra credit. Most of you probably aren't in need of a credit counsellor's intervention. But do you know how creditworthy you are? Your FICO credit score is calculated by the Fair Isaac Corporation (named after founders Bill Fair and

Keep in mind that whoever you choose should be credited with 100 percent of the amount you pay through a credit-counselling agency. (Translation: Make sure the *entire* debt payment you send to the agency is going towards your balance.) And remember, while a credit counsellor can help to renegotiate your monthly payments, your interest rate, and sometimes even the amount you must repay to avoid defaulting on your debt, the repayment plan may be noted on your credit report for years to come. You might also get into trouble if the agency you work with sends in one of your payments late. Before you enlist the help of an outside agency, try calling your creditors directly to explain your financial situation and see if you can work out a payment plan that you're able to afford. If that doesn't work, a credit counsellor may be able to negotiate more successfully for lower rates. But be sure to ask what steps you can take to minimize any long-term damage to your credit.

Earl Isaac) based on information from each credit reporting agency—that's why you may have a slightly different score depending on the agency through which you get your score—and can range from about 300 to 850. Fair Isaac uses a proprietary formula. But we'll let you in on some of the factors it uses to crunch the numbers and how much weight is given to each. Here's how your FICO score breaks down:

- 35 percent = payment history
- 30 percent = amounts owed on each account
- 15 percent = length of credit (how long you've had the accounts)
- 10 percent = new credit (new accounts opened or inquiries made for more credit)
- 10 percent = types of credit in use (e.g. credit card, department store, mortgage, or school loans)

There are simple ways to improve your score in each category.

Payment History
- Pay your monthly payments on time.
- If you are having trouble keeping up with payments, notify your lender that you need to work out an arrangement and then get current on any past-due accounts as soon as possible.

Amounts Owed
- Keep low balances relative to your credit limit: Keeping your total balance at 35 percent or less than your total credit available is good, though, of course, a zero balance is best.
- The level of revolving debt (like credit cards) is one of the most important factors in determining your FICO score. The credit agencies look at your total balances in relation to your total available credit, as well as the balances on your individual revolving accounts. Opening new accounts just to make your outstanding balances look smaller in relation to your total credit capacity won't help; in fact, it could actually hurt if

you rack up more debt on those accounts. Opening too many new lines of credit, even if you don't use them, could also lower your FICO score. (Agencies get suspicious when you apply for an excessive amount of credit in a particular period.)

Length of Credit

- Consider keeping old accounts open if you've been a good borrower. Instead of improving your credit, as you might think, closing an account actually erases your good payment history from your report (assuming you had a good history and didn't miss or fall behind on any payments). So erasing the card can actually hurt your credit history, which is a critical factor in determining your score. You can cut up the card but leave the account alone.

New Credit Category

- Credit agencies look at how many accounts you've recently opened compared with your total number of accounts, as well as the number of recent inquiries made by lenders to whom you've applied for credit. That means your score can drop if it looks like you're seeking several new sources of credit in a short time period—a sign that you may be in financial trouble. (If a lender initiates an inquiry about your credit report without your knowledge, though, it shouldn't affect your score.) Shopping around for an auto loan or mortgage shouldn't hurt. But every inquiry you trigger when you apply for a credit card can affect your score, so keep those to a minimum.
- If you already have a bad history, you can improve your credit score by opening a new credit card and managing it responsibly and paying off the balance each month. Find a card you like and then apply for it, though, rather than sending in multiple applications. The Financial Consumer Agency of Canada (www.fcac-acfc.gc.ca) is a great resource for comparing the features and rates of various cards, or try www.creditcards.ca.

Types of Credit

- Having so-called "installment" debt (where you pay fixed monthly installments to eliminate the debt, like a mortgage) is considered better than having "revolving" debt, like credit card balances.
- Be aware that having certain finance company debts (like using retailer financing to buy furniture or other big-ticket items) is also less desirable than having a mortgage or other "installment" debts.

Before she joined the Smart Cookies, Robyn says she missed credit card payments all the time. She often sent off payments towards her credit card balances whenever she had a little extra money, with no regard to due dates. The only time she would send a sizable payment was when she wanted to make a large purchase and needed to increase the available credit on her card to do so. Not surprisingly, her credit score suffered from her erratic payments. She didn't know how badly until she applied for a mortgage and was told politely that her credit "wasn't great." In order to qualify for a loan with a reasonable interest rate, her mortgage broker had to send a letter of recommendation to her lender, explaining how she was trying to pay down her debts and improve her credit. Fortunately, the bank relented and she was able to qualify for a mortgage with a payment she could afford. But she was determined not to let her credit score slip again.

Always keep a close eye on your credit score, as it has a direct impact on your ability to take out a mortgage, credit card or other loan and on the interest you'll pay for it. We recommend that you each get a copy of your credit report and your score to have on hand, so that you know where you stand and where you need to make improvements. Remember that requesting a copy of your credit report or score does NOT affect your credit score, no matter how many requests you make or how often, as long as you order it directly from a credit-reporting agency or through an organization that's authorized to provide reports to consumers (versus a credit card offer that promises to give you a free credit report if you apply for a card). You can also call your card company to see if it offers free access to track your score.

If you do notice changes in your score or report, call the credit bureau that issued the score or report and ask for an explanation. If there are errors on your report, you can submit a request to correct them. Before the credit-reporting agency can make a correction on your credit report, it must contact the financial institution that reported the information to see if an error was made.

According to the Financial Consumer Agency of Canada, if the financial institution agrees that an error was made, the credit-reporting agency has 30 days (with the exception of Alberta, which allows 90 days) to correct your credit report. If the financial institution says that the information reported is correct, but you are still not satisfied, you can also submit a brief statement to the credit-reporting agency that explains your situation. This statement will be added to your credit report.

smart bite

TAKING CREDIT. No matter how you decide to divvy up the financial responsibilities with your partner, be sure to have at least one bank account and debit/credit card in your own name. This is not only important in establishing credit in your name, but it allows you to have some money for personal expenses and for investments that your partner may not want to make with your joint funds. Robyn had no credit in her own name when she was married. And though she and her husband had a joint line of credit of $80,000 when they were together, she was unable to get more than $500 in her name alone after they split up (even though she had almost $120,000 invested into her home!).

Step Six:

Don't wait to invest. You don't need to put *every* available dollar towards your debts until they're all paid off. Sometimes investing some of that money instead can make better financial sense. Maybe you've been able to transfer your credit card balance or negotiate your rate down to a 1.99- or 2.99-percent APR (annual percentage rate), but you can make more than that in interest with a money market account or a GIC (Guaranteed Investment Certificate). You want to continue to pay off your debt, but you could also put some of your money into the interest-bearing account or GIC. This way you'll actually be earning more than you're paying in interest on your debt. In the summer of 2009, banks were offering rates of 3 percent or more on three- to five-year GICs.

You may also want to use some of the money you've saved towards a down payment on a home, instead of paying off a debt. If the price is good—and prices are pretty low right now—and you plan to stay in your home for a while, the decision may pay off. But you want to be sure that your monthly mortgage payments aren't so high that it keeps you from being able to pay down that debt quickly. We'll go into more detail on how to calculate how much you should put towards a down payment, versus a debt, in the next chapter.

Smart Cookie Summary

Discussion Questions:

1.   How much debt do you each have and what types are you carrying?
2.   How much are you paying in interest on each of your balances?
3.   Do you want to pay off your debts together, or are you each responsible for your personal debts?
4.   What are your credit scores?
5.   What are some steps you can take now to improve your scores?

Smart Steps:

1. Add up all of your debts and discuss whether you want to pay them off together or on your own.
2. Prioritize your payments by focusing on "bad" high-interest balances first.
3. Try to negotiate lower rates or transfer your balances to a low-interest card (or pay them off with a low-interest loan).
4. Order your credit score and credit report, and submit requests to fix any errors on your report.
5. Decide whether it makes more sense to pay off all your balances first, or to pay some off more slowly and invest some of your savings.

chapter 7

Don't Sweat the Big Stuff

What to Know Before Buying a Home or Starting a Family

Buying a home and starting a family. After marriage, they're two of the most common rites of passage for committed couples. They're also two of the biggest expenses of your life. So you want to be certain that you're financially prepared before you do either.

In this chapter, we'll give you all the information you need to make sure you're ready. In the first section, we focus on the financial costs, and benefits, of starting a family. In the second section, we tell you everything you need to know about buying a home—and one that's not just a place to live but a long-term investment.

Your home will probably be the most expensive one-time purchase you ever make. And it can also be one of the best investments. Among us, we have invested in close to $1 million worth of real estate, and we've all seen our homes appreciate in value. True, we bought well before the real estate bubble popped, and the market is certainly not the same today as it was when we purchased our homes, but over the long term, housing values have historically increased and they're expected to do so again in the future. In fact, now might be a great time to buy since prices are so low. Regardless of the market, do your research first. We'll tell you what you need to know to make sure you're getting the best deal—and not getting in over your head—and what you should look for in a home to ensure it will appreciate in value.

First, though, let's focus on family. We understand that not everyone wants kids, of course. But if you do, this section is for you. We don't need to tell you about the benefits of starting a family; the ways in which children can enrich your lives are immeasurable. Fortunately, the costs of raising them *are* measurable, so you can get a good idea of what to expect even before you're, well, expecting. We'll help you calculate how much you need to save and to earn to raise a family in Canada today, and show you some ways you can cut those expenses without cutting corners.

Bringing Up Baby

One reason that having a baby can seem so expensive is that you're often hit with a double whammy financially. Your household income is likely to go down since one of you will stop working (at least temporarily), and at the same time your expenses are increasing. That's why it's so important to make sure you've got enough savings to help get you through your baby's first year—at the very least. The good news is, the first year is often the toughest one financially—and physically and mentally, too, many new parents would argue, as you're still adjusting to parenthood and working your way up the learning curve. So keep in mind that things should get a little easier after your baby's first birthday, assuming you don't encounter other financial hardships like a job loss or an unexpected car repair. (The fact that you might, though, is a good reason to keep a little extra in that savings account.) In general, the older your kids get, the lower your annual expenses should be—at least until they go to college.

So how much do you need to save to make sure you're well prepared?

According to the most recent report by Manitoba Agriculture, you can expect to spend more than $166,000 to raise a child from birth to age 18. The first is typically the most expensive, costing the average parents nearly $10,100 in extra expenses. The cost of child care accounts for nearly half of that estimate at around $4,500, followed by the cost of furnishings (think a crib, bassinet, and changing table) and the amount you'll pay for additional usage of utilities like electricity and water (Hello laundry!); clothing; and food. One expense that's typically lower for younger children is health care, which costs less than $150 on average in the first year. And of course, your expenses can vary depending on where you live in Canada.

An informal 2009 survey of parents by the CBC found that the average daycare costs ranged from $600 to $1,300 *a month* per child in Toronto, while in Montreal—where there are more subsidized options available—the cost ranged from $150 to about $700 per month per child. (The CBC found that by 2004, there were more than 745,000 regulated daycare spaces across Canada, but nearly half of them were in Quebec. More than half of the children in daycare in Quebec were getting subsidized tuition.)

A Calgary couple, profiled in *Today's Parent*, who have a five-year-old and a two-year-old, said they paid $1,440 a month for child care, or more than $700 per child. Another couple in Kitchener, Ontario, with a three-year-old and a one-year-old, said they were spending about $1,100 a month on child care. Since there's such a wide range in tuition costs, it's best to do some research ahead of time to find out whether you're likely to get your child into a subsidized daycare in your area—or if such a thing exists. Check to see how the costs of daycare compare to those related to hiring a nanny, which can run about $250 or more a week for a live-in, depending on how many kids you have. In an ideal world, one way to save money is to hire a part-time sitter and try to enlist the help of a nearby relative to watch your baby one or two days a week— and then your child is spending quality time with family, too. Claire and Ryan, the Toronto couple with a newborn, have enlisted the help of both grandmothers to help watch their baby after Claire returns to work as a schoolteacher. That will help them cut their child care expenses considerably, and both of their mothers are thrilled with it!

After child care, here are some of the top monthly expenses and some tips for saving money on each.

Furnishings

Estimated Cost: $300 to $800.

How to Save: Many stores sell matching furniture sets, which often include a chest, drawers, and maybe an armoire, and can cost $1,000 or more (though they are more reasonable at stores like Ikea. But that doesn't mean you have to buy them. Focus on what you need. Buy a sturdy new crib, which you can find for under $250 (though don't forget to tack on another $100 or so for bedding), and a diaper changing table, which costs between $100 and $200. And pass on the non-essential items. Instead of an expensive trunk, consider buying fabric or plastic bins for storage. When you're looking at cribs, consider one that adapts as your child grows, converting from a crib to a toddler bed to a daybed. That can save you money down the road. Look for changing tables that are sturdy, have a protective guardrail, and offer storage for diapers, wipes, and creams. Changing pads and pad covers range from about $10 to $50. Pads should come with safety straps.

Diapers

Estimated Cost: $50 to $100 per month, depending on how quickly you go through a pack.

How to Save: Buy them in bulk at wholesale clubs like Costco. Use generic store brands. Sign up at diaper manufacturers' websites to get coupons. Stock up when diapers are on sale. Stores like Babies "R" Us offer coupons periodically on a variety of basic baby items, including diapers. Just sign up at the store to receive the coupons by mail.

Feeding

Estimated cost: $100+ per month for those who are bottle feeding exclusively.

How to Save: Breastfeeding is one obvious way to spend less on formula. Just keep in mind that breast pumps can be expensive (try renting instead of buying) if you're pumping milk. Not breastfeeding? Then opt for a powdered formula, which costs less than the ready-to-use or liquid concentrate versions. Again, it pays to buy in bulk at warehouse stores like Costco. You can also sign up to get coupons through the formula manufacturers' websites. One tip: On some sites, your relatives can also sign up to get coupons then forward them on to you. (Just make sure they don't mind getting the flyers and promotions that also come in the mail when you sign up.)

Baby Essentials

Estimated Cost: A few hundred dollars to a few thousand, depending on the brands and models you pick (and whether you get them used or new).

How to Save: List some of the basics on your baby registry, so that your friends and family can pitch in on big-ticket items like a car seat, a reliable stroller, and a high chair (consider one that converts to a toddler chair and table). Then ask for hand-me-downs from friends with kids who've outgrown them. Some items to consider: bassinets, Pack 'n Plays, baby bathtubs, and age-specific activity gear like bouncy chairs or saucers. You can also post a request for used items on local parenting sites or on craigslist. You can often get great deals on barely used gear. If a baby has outgrown something, or doesn't seem interested in it, parents are only too eager to keep it from taking up space. Also keep in mind that, with some items, the difference in quality is not always a reflection of the difference in price. You can get a quality stroller, for example, for $200 or less, though some designer strollers cost as much as $800 new. In some cases, you may be paying more for the label. (If you can find a stroller that's gently used, you can often get a good deal. Just be sure to inspect it before you buy it, as wear and tear can affect the quality of a stroller.) Sites like viewpoints.com (www.viewpoints.com/Strollers) and eBay.ca offer reviews and price comparisons for a variety of makes and models. The Transport Canada site (www.tc.gc.ca) has tips for choosing and installing car seats and information on product recalls.

Clothing

Estimated Cost: $50 to $100 per month.

How to Save: *Consumer Reports* recommends putting together a beginner wardrobe of a dozen T-shirts and one-piece outfits. (You can do this for less than $150.) Then add items as you need them. Buy shirts, pants, and PJs in a size that's six months ahead of your baby's age so you can use them longer. (Just make sure the pants have an elastic waistband so they don't slip off; then roll up the cuffs.) You can always roll up the sleeves and pant legs until they fit. One exception is pajamas, which should be tighter fitting (especially those with footies). Sale. Sale. Sale. Don't get sidetracked by the expensive stuff. Basic, good-quality, and often stylish infant outfits can cost as little as $12 or less at stores like Old Navy, The Gap, Walmart, and H&M. In general, avoid displays in front and head for the sales items in back. Don't forget to scour second-hand shops and ask for hand-me-downs from friends. Babies grow so quickly, the clothes have often just been worn a few times and can look new. Stephanie and Eric, our couple in San Francisco, estimated they spend about $80 or less per month on clothes for both their children in part because their younger son has gotten so many quality hand-me-downs from older boys in the neighbourhood.

Want more information? Babycenter.com has a first-year baby cost calculator, using information from a survey of what 1,000 new moms spent on various items (www.babycenter.com/babyCostCalculator.htm).

Baby Benefits

When it comes to having children, planning is key. Another way to offset the costs of raising a child is to take advantage of some of the tax deductions, tax credits, and other benefits offered by the federal and provincial governments. You may not qualify for all of these, but you'll certainly be eligible for some. Make sure to apply as early as you can, as it takes time to process the applications.

• **Universal Child Care Benefit (UCCB)** is a government program that offers Canadian families $100 (pre-tax) each month per child under the age of six, to be used, ostensibly towards *any* child care costs—but your baby does not need to be in a daycare for you to receive this benefit. Make sure to apply for this as soon as possible after giving birth, as the first payments may not arrive for up to three months after you apply.

• **Goods and Services Tax (GST) Credit** is a federal credit designed to assist lower- and modest-income Canadians. The amount is based on a combination of family size and income.

• **Canada Child Tax Benefit (CCTB)** is aimed at low- and middle-income families. The amount is based on the age and number of children, family income, and child care expenses. Benefits are paid monthly and are non-taxable. There is a basic benefit for each child under 18. Call 1-800-387-1193 for more information.

• **The Child Disability Benefit (CDB)** is a tax-free benefit paid out monthly for families with a child under the age of 18 who has "a severe and prolonged impairment in mental or physical functions," which lasts at least 12 months.

Note: There are income thresholds for the CCTB and CDB. For the 2009–2010 benefit year, the family net income threshold at which both begin to be phased out was expected to increase to about $40,726. You can get information and applications for these credits and benefits through the Canada Revenue Agency site (www.cra-arc.gc.ca).

• **Employment Insurance Maternity Benefits (a.k.a. Maternity Leave)** are available to new moms (or surrogates) who have worked at least 600 hours during the previous 52 weeks. You can get up to 55 percent of your average insured earnings up to a yearly maximum of $42,300 (or about $450 a week). Just remember that this is taxable income, and you can only collect it up to 17 weeks (depending on the province, though it can be combined with parental benefits so you're paid for a total of 52 weeks—see below). But you can start getting the benefits up to 8 weeks before you give birth. So apply early. Call 1-800-206-7218 for more information.

• **Employment Insurance Parental Benefits** are payable either to the biological or adoptive parents while they're caring for a newborn or an adopted child. These last up to a maximum of 37 weeks. You can tack them onto the smart bite

GET A HEAD START ON COLLEGE SAVINGS. It's never too early to start saving for college. Compared to the United States, the cost of higher education is a relative bargain in Canada. But tuition costs have been rising about 4.4 percent per year over the last decade. In the 2008–2009 school year, full-time students in undergraduate programs paid on average more than $4,700 per annum, while graduate students paid close to $5,800. The costs were even higher for some undergrad specialties: Undergraduate students in dentistry paid more than $12,900 in undergraduate fees, while students in medicine paid close to $10,400 on average.

That's a pretty big bill—especially if you have to pay it annually for four years or more. But you can make it much more manageable by setting up a Registered Education Savings Plan (RESP), a government-registered plan that helps you save now for a child's education after high school. A few points to keep in mind are:

- You need to have social insurance numbers for yourself and your child to set up an RESP.
- You can invest as much as you want per year, up to the maximum lifetime contribution of $50,000 per child.
- All gains in the plan are tax deferred, so your money grows tax free. When the funds are withdrawn, they're taxed to the student you listed as the beneficiary. But since students tend to have little or no income, they aren't likely to pay much in taxes on their withdrawals.
- If your child decides not to go on to college or university, you should get all your money back along with the income earned on it, but you'll have to pay taxes on your earnings.
- The plans are offered by most banks and credit unions, as well as group plan dealers and some certified financial planners. Just be

aware that some RESP providers charge service fees, and some may also impose restrictions on the amount of money you can put into your plan and how often you can contribute. So choose carefully.

Want to make your money grow even faster? The Canadian government's Canada Education Savings Grant (CESG) matches up to 20 percent of your annual contributions. There are some income restrictions though. On the first $500 you saved in your child's RESP in 2009, for example, the grant would contribute:

- up to $200, if your net annual family income was $38,832 or less
- up to $150, if your net family income was between $38,832 and $77,664
- up to $100, if your net family income was more than $77,664

When you save more than $500 annually, the Canada Education Savings Grant could add up to $400 on the next $2,000. But keep in mind that the family income limits are updated every year, and the maximum amount of the grant per child was $7,200, as of mid-2009.

You may also qualify for a Canada Learning Bond, which provides up to $2,000 plus interest in bonds to be used for your child's education. In order to qualify, your child must have been born in 2004 or later, and you need to get the National Child Benefit Supplement as part of the Canada Child Tax Benefit, which usually applies to families whose annual net income is below $39,000.

To apply for the grant or bond, make sure to sign up with an RESP provider who offers them. The Canadian government provides more information at www.canlearn.ca.

maternity benefits (meaning you could collect benefits for up to 52 weeks) or share them with your spouse. To get the parental benefits, you must show you've worked at least 600 hours in the last year. Go to the Service Canada site for more info (www.servicecanada.gc.ca).

• **Child Care Deductions** You may be able to deduct child care expenses from your income when you're filling out your tax return, so make sure to keep receipts for your child care expenses—from nannies to nursery schools, day and overnight camps. You may also claim child care expenses paid to allow you or your spouse to go to school part-time. As of 2009, you could claim up to $7,000 annually per child under the age of seven, and up to $4,000 for those between seven and 16 years old. The Canada Revenue Agency site has more information on the deductions (www.cra-arc.gc.ca).

Home $weet Home

As expensive as it is to raise a child, the cost of owning a home is usually even higher—from a purely monetary perspective. But there can be big pay-offs too, as long as you choose wisely and pick a home you can afford. At the least, you get a roof over your head and you start building equity (the current market value of your home minus what you still owe on your mortgage), but it can also be a very lucrative step. As long as the value stays steady or increases by the time you sell, you can make back what you paid and, hopefully, more. In some cases, your home could increase sharply in value—as happened to many who bought and sold their homes between 2000 and 2006—and you could make a bundle. Andrea made more than $120,000 from selling her home just about two years after she bought it! Of course, that was a few years ago, and a lot has changed since then. If you were unlucky enough to buy at the peak, you may actually find you owe more than your home is worth right now. But remember that real estate is cyclical. You can generally expect the value of your home to go up over several years. Buying real estate is one of the few purchases you can make in which you're nearly assured that the product you bought will be worth more, not less, in the future—at least, over the long run.

Think of it this way: You have to live somewhere, so why pay for someone else's mortgage instead of your own? When you rent, you're basically paying for the privilege of staying in that space for the next month, and paying someone else's mortgage. Sure, you're generally not responsible for covering the cost of repairs or maintenance, but when your lease is up, you've got nothing to show for it. When you own, part of each monthly payment usually goes towards your principal (the amount you owe to cover the price of the home when you bought it, minus the mortgage payments you've made) and the other part goes to cover the interest on your loan. When the mortgage is paid off, you've actually got something to show for it: a home that you own free and clear—even though it might take a few years! And though you are responsible for repairs and upkeep, improvements you make to your home can actually help boost its resale value, so you can often recoup some or all of the costs when you sell your home. (We'll give you tips on which renovations are most likely to increase the value of your home later in this chapter.)

We know firsthand how valuable real estate can be. Four of us have purchased homes and have seen our investments appreciate, and Angela is a licensed realtor. Four of us have purchased homes and have seen our investments appreciate. Yes, the real estate market has declined recently. But that doesn't mean you should put off purchasing a home—in fact, this might be a great time to buy, since prices are low. You just need to plan on staying in it for a while longer before selling it, if you want to make a profit. And make sure to do your research before buying it so that you know you are able to afford the down payment *plus* the mortgage and any taxes or maintenance fees, and that the property you buy is not overvalued and is likely to increase in value (at least, over the long run).

In this section, we'll give you a checklist to follow before you purchase real estate and we'll share stories of how we found and bought our homes. Drawing from our own experience and from Angela's expertise as a realtor, we'll also reveal some secrets on how to save money when purchasing a new home, what criteria to look for in buying a home, and what renovations and upgrades are worth making and will bring the most value when you resell.

Before You Buy . . .

Know What You Can Afford

Having a realistic idea of how much you can afford to spend—both on the down payment, and all related closing costs, plus the monthly mortgage payments—will save you a lot of time and heartache in your search for the right place. Get your finances in order before you start your house hunt. Make sure you speak with a lender to find out exactly what you can afford: not just in terms of the money you can put towards a down payment, but the amount you'll be paying every month on the mortgage and other related expenses. Lenders will add up your estimated housing costs to figure out what percentage they are of your gross monthly income, a figure known as your Gross Debt Service (GDS) ratio. Generally speaking, those monthly housing costs—including mortgage principal and interest, taxes, and heating expenses—shouldn't be more than 32 percent of your gross household monthly income, according to the Canada Mortgage and Housing Corporation (CMHC). The agency also suggests that your *entire* monthly debt, including housing costs and other debts like credit card payments, student loans, and car loans, shouldn't be more than 40 percent of your gross monthly income.

To figure out 32 percent of your gross monthly income, multiply your annual gross salary by 0.32 then divide by 12. So, for example, let's say you each make 50,000 annually before taxes, or about $8,330 combined per month, 32 percent of that would be about $2,667 a month. You'd generally want to make sure that you won't end up paying more than that between the mortgage payment and other monthly costs, when you consider what you can afford. Note: In expensive areas like Toronto, Vancouver, and Calgary, where real estate prices are much higher than the national average, residents do tend to spend a higher percentage of their income on housing. But that doesn't mean you should. If you're living in a high-cost market, it may make sense to rent a little longer—if your rent is less than you would pay for a monthly mortgage for a comparably-sized place—and pay off all your debts and save some additional money before you take on a hefty monthly mortgage payment.

Don't forget to factor in the other upfront costs of buying a home like:

- **Mortgage Loan Insurance Premium.** If you're putting less than 20 percent down on a home, your lender may need mortgage loan insurance. Ask if you can add the mortgage insurance premium to your mortgage or if you have to pay it in full upon closing.
- **Appraisal Fee.** Your mortgage lender may require that the property be appraised at your expense. The cost for an appraisal, or an estimate of the value of the home, may cost between $250 and $350.
- **Deposit.** This is part of your down payment, but it must be paid when you make the initial Offer to Purchase. The amount can vary depending on the area, but it may be up to 5 percent of the purchase price.
- **Home Inspection Fee.** CMHC recommends that you make a home inspection a condition of your Offer to Purchase. A home inspection is a report on the condition of the home and can cost around $500, depending on what the inspection includes.
- **Property Insurance.** The mortgage lender generally requires this because the home is security for the mortgage. This insurance covers the cost of replacing your home and its contents and, typically, must be in place on the day you close.
- **Survey or Certificate of Location Cost.** The mortgage lender may ask for an up-to-date survey or certificate of location prior to finalizing the mortgage loan. If the seller doesn't have one, you may have to pay for it yourself, which can set you back $1,000 to $2,000.
- **Legal Fees and Disbursements.** These have to be paid upon closing and generally cost a minimum of $500. Your lawyer or notary can also bill you for the costs to check on the legal status of your property.
- **Title Insurance.** A "title" is the legal term for ownership of a property. A title search is typically conducted before you close on a property to make sure that there are no liens against the home, for example, from

previous owners. But sometimes problems regarding title are not discovered before closing. So your lender or lawyer or notary may suggest
title insurance to cover any problems that come up later that may make
your property less marketable and cost money to fix. The amount of
title insurance you need is based on the value of your home and the
amount of your mortgage. Also, count on a one-time fee for the policy,
usually paid at closing.

- **Property Transfer Tax.** This is generally calculated as 1 percent of the
first $200,000 of the fair market value of the property, plus 2 percent
of the remaining fair market value of the transaction.

Be aware that a big credit card balance could also limit the size of the mortgage loan that you'll be able to attain. Before you apply for a mortgage, try to pay
off as many outstanding balances as possible. That will help improve your credit
scores and your overall debt-to-income ratio (or how much you owe each month
versus how much you make). Then you may qualify for a lower interest rate on
your mortgage, which can save you tens of thousands of dollars over the course
of your loan repayment. If your partner has a much better score than you do, or
vice versa, it may be tempting just to submit that person's information on the
mortgage application. But remember that means you're only submitting one
person's income and assets, too. So you probably won't qualify to borrow nearly
as much as you would together. Also, ultimately, don't you want both of your
names on the mortgage? You'll both be responsible for paying it, after all.

Going through the pre-approval process with your bank or a mortgage
broker is a good exercise to ensure that you'll be able to afford the mortgage
payments and related costs. But remember that just because you've been
approved for a specific mortgage does *not* mean you need to purchase a house
for that dollar figure. The last thing you want to be is house poor (meaning
that so much of your disposable income is going towards your house, you can't
afford the other important things you want in your life). Once you've calculated the monthly payments and upfront costs you can afford, pick a price
range and stick with it.

smart SC bite

SOME HELP FOR FIRST-TIME HOMEBUYERS. The government offers some programs that may make it easier for you to buy your first home now. The new Home Buyers' Tax Credit (HBTC), which was added to the 2009 budget, will provide up to $750 for Canadians who purchased their first home after January 27, 2009. (The amount may go up in 2010 and beyond.) The Home Buyers' Plan (HBP) was also updated to allow first-time homebuyers to withdraw up to $25,000 from your registered retirement savings plan (RRSPs) to buy or build a home, as long as it will be your principal residence within one year of buying or building it. (Once you occupy the home, though, there is no minimum period of time that you have to live there.) Keep in mind that if you're buying the house together, that means each one of you is allowed to take out up to $25,000 from your RRSPs to put towards the home. Just remember that this is considered a temporary "loan" from your RRSP. You each must pay back the amount you borrow from your RRSP within 15 years or it will be added to your taxable income.

If you're buying your first home, you may also be exempt from paying a property transfer tax (PTT), which can potentially cost in the thousands. Apply for the exemption yourself if you register the property at the land title offices, or have a lawyer or notary public apply for the exemption on your behalf. To qualify, you need to occupy the property within 92 days of the date you registered it, or had it registered, and use it as your principal residence for at least a year. (If you do not apply for the exemption when you register the property at the land title offices, you can apply for a refund of the property transfer tax you pay within 18 months of the date you registered the property.)

Decide on a Down Payment

How much money do you need to put down to buy a home? Though there are some exceptions, lenders generally prefer a down payment of at least 20 percent. Don't forget that you'll be paying interest on whatever amount you borrow. So the more money you're able to put into a down payment, the better. The difference can save you thousands of dollars in interest.

If either or both of you have debt, you may be wondering: Should we pay off our debt first or save some cash for a down payment and buy a home now?

Lenders often use debt-to-income ratio guidelines when they're assessing your ability to cover your housing costs. They look at how much of your gross (meaning pre-tax) monthly income would be used towards housing costs. Then they examine the minimum you owe each month on your credit cards, car or school loans and other debt obligations). Though the guidelines can be flexible, depending on your credit, your bank, and the type of loan you're getting, the general rule of thumb is that debt and housing expenses combined should be no more than 40 percent of your monthly pre-tax income. So what does that mean for you?

Let's take the same example we used earlier. If you each make about $50,000 a year in pre-tax salary, or about $8,330 combined per month, ideally, you shouldn't be paying more than about $665 in monthly minimum payments towards your debt if you're planning to buy a home now (or about 8 percent). If you owe much more than that per month on your credit cards, credit line, car or school loans, you probably should be putting your money towards your debt first and put off buying real estate until you're able to pay off some of your debts. Few banks would give you a loan—or, at least, one with a good interest rate—if your debt payments are much higher than this. On the other hand, if you each make $50,000 but owe less than 5 percent of your pre-tax monthly income, your debt probably won't affect your ability to get a mortgage with a desirable interest rate (assuming you have good credit). Though you should have a plan in place to pay down your debt, in this case it might make more sense to put extra savings you have now towards a down payment instead.

Why aim for a 20-percent down payment? Typically lenders will require mortgage loan insurance if you put down less than that. The insurance, which your lender generally applies for through the CMHC on your behalf, is intended to ensure that the lender will not lose money if you do not make your mortgage payments and the property value is not high enough to repay the mortgage debt. The insurance is paid to the lender and is generally blended in with your mortgage payments.

We understand, though, that 20 percent down is not always realistic. It may be worth it for you to put down less and pay for the insurance. Your lender should be able to tell you how many years and months it will take you to pay down your loan enough to cancel the mortgage insurance (if you have a fixed-rate mortgage), so you'll be able to factor that into your calculations for the homes you can afford

Research Real Estate Values

Can you be sure that real estate values will increase in your area? No. At least not in the short term, as many recent homebuyers have learned the hard way.

Prices have slipped over the past couple of years across Canada, though there is some evidence that the tide is starting to turn—at least, in some areas. The Royal LePage Survey of Canadian House Prices, which includes information on seven types of housing in more than 250 neighbourhoods, found prices in most provinces fell between the first quarter of 2008 and the first quarter of 2009, with two-storey homes in Canada declining 6.5 percent in price on average and condo prices falling about 4 percent. The one exception was Newfoundland, where prices actually went up. But in May, the Canadian Real Estate Association reported that the average price of existing homes sold nationwide had actually increased, though by less than half a percent. And some provinces, like British Columbia, saw prices fall further.

The good news for you, if you're thinking of buying your first home, is that the low prices mean it's a buyer's market. Even if prices fall a bit further in the next year or two, you should still come out ahead if you're planning to stick it out for the long term. This can be a great time to buy. In many areas, owners who need to sell may be willing to accept bids that are significantly lower than the initial asking price. If you see a home you love that's been for sale for months, you may be able to negotiate a price that's thousands of dollars lower than the one initially listed. Just make sure to check the recent sales prices of other homes in the area to ensure you're not paying more than market value.

Remember, real estate markets are cyclical, but over time, on average, housing prices have historically gone up, not down. Hold on to your home for a while and you're still likely to see the value appreciate.

There are certain criteria you should look for when you buy a new home, though, to help ensure that its value will increase over the long run.

Location, Location, Location

As you and your partner explore various neighbourhoods, ask yourselves: Is it reasonable to expect that this community will still be an attractive place to live in five, ten, or even fifteen years? Is it an up-and-coming area or an established community? How well is it maintained? Are the streets well lit and well paved? Are there public parks? How do graduation and college acceptance rates and test scores in the local school system compare to those in nearby districts? (Even if you don't have kids, schools play a big part in the resale value of a home.) How do the local crime statistics compare to the national average and to other nearby communities? In addition to residential neighbourhoods, does the community have an appealing mix of commercial and business development? Are there local restaurants and shops you and your partner can enjoy—places you'd be proud to show off to houseguests? Are there basic services nearby like a dry cleaner, a grocery store, and a pharmacy? Check into development plans around your property. Are there many empty lots? Are there plans for more homes or nearby restaurants or other attractions? With the recent drop in the market, some plans may be on hold. So beware of empty lots and half-built properties nearby. It might be a long time before they're transformed into something more than an eyesore. Research the neighbourhood statistics online, read about what goes on in the community, and talk with your realtor and with residents who live in the area. You should also talk to a realtor about which of these criteria tend to be most important to buyers in general, so you get an idea of how these could affect the value of the home you buy in the future.

Take Taxes Into Account

Property taxes fluctuate from community to community. While higher property taxes can often mean newer schools, well-maintained roads, and better community services, prospective buyers may be turned off by the thought of higher costs no matter what the amenities—particularly if neighbouring areas have lower taxes. And you may be, too. Don't forget to figure taxes into the equation when you're calculating how much you can afford. Take some time to talk about this with your partner and prioritize your needs.

Size Matters

But not in the way you think it does. If you're concerned about resale value, you probably do *not* want to buy the largest model in the neighbourhood. If most of the nearby houses are smaller than your house, they can actually drag down the value of yours. On the other hand, if you buy a house that's small or medium-sized for the neighbourhood, the larger homes around it can help pull up the value of yours. If you want to make sure your home appreciates, it's smarter to buy a smaller home in a better neighbourhood than to buy a bigger one in a less desirable neighbourhood. *Focus on features. Focus on features.*

Before you even start looking for a home, it is essential to take the time to agree on the features you can and can't live without, and then write up a list. Keep in mind those features that might add to the home's value—like a walk-in closet, a two-car garage, lots of light, and hardwood floors—and which may take away from it (few windows, awkward-shaped rooms, outdated fixtures and appliances). It may be helpful for each of you to list five to ten features that you like and prioritize them. That can help you narrow down your search and prevent you from wasting time looking at homes that don't really meet your criteria. Plus, by discussing what you each want before you start looking, you can help avoid potential conflicts later.

When Andrea was deciding which condo to purchase, for example, she narrowed it down to one that had a walk-in closet in the master bedroom and a conventional kitchen, and another with granite countertops and stainless steel appliances in the kitchen but little closet space. Both the fancy kitchen and the walk-in closet would be attractive to future buyers, if or when she chose to resell her condo. But Andrea decided that having the larger closet was more important to her than having stainless steel appliances. An up-to-date kitchen helps boost a home's value. But if you plan on living in your home for a while, you may end up renovating the kitchen anyway.

In some cases, it may be worth paying for renovations yourself at some point. If a home has an outdated kitchen, you may be able to negotiate a better price and use some of the savings to make improvements and install new appliances later on. Then you'll have a personalized kitchen *and* a house that's worth more! A 2007 report by Hanley Wood L.L.C., a media company that serves the housing sector, and *REALTOR* magazine found that kitchen remodelling was the best value among indoor renovations, returning 83 percent of the costs on average (meaning that if the kitchen upgrade cost $10,000, it boosted the home's value by $8,300).

If you're buying a condo or apartment, there are other considerations that might be important to you both too. If you're buying a unit in a large building, ask each other whether it's important that the building have a concierge, an elevator, a gym, extra storage, or access to common areas like a roof deck or garden. Maybe you're willing to forego an elevator for a better-priced condo or one with a nicer view. But keep in mind that even if you're fit enough to climb four flights of stairs every day, prospective future buyers may not be. And if you're planning a family, don't forget to take that into account as well. You're buying for the long term so you want to think about your future needs as well as your current ones.

Find the Right Real Estate Agent

It's important to take the time to find a realtor who really understands your financial situation, your timeline, and the qualities you're both looking for in a home. You want someone who will work with you through every step of the home-buying process, representing your interests, and getting you the best deal possible on the home you want. You want someone who knows the area well and will lend his or her experience and knowledge to help narrow your search for the right home, and who will not push you to buy a home you cannot afford. It's a good idea to get referrals from friends or family members who have bought or sold a home recently. If you opt to use the Internet instead to find an agent in your area, seek out well-established real estate companies then look up profiles of individual agents until you find one who seems like a good fit. You can also ask for references from previous clients.

When selecting someone to represent you in the purchase of your home you want to look for someone with the Realtor® trademark. This can only be used by those who are members of the Canadian Real Estate Association. A Realtor® must abide by and respect a strict code of ethics. The association's code of ethics is a comprehensive list of 28 articles detailing standards of practice that go above and beyond those required by law. You can get more info at www.howrealtorshelp.ca (a site run by the Canadian Real Estate Association).

Look for Undervalued Properties

Before you start looking for a home in a particular area, do some research on average home prices so that you'll be able to spot an undervalued property. The Canadian Real Estate Association website is a good resource to find information on the current housing market and also to look at the trends for housing prices and units sold. You can do searches by street or neighbourhood at www.realtor.ca. The Teranet-National Bank House Price Index also provides average home price changes in six metropolitan areas: Ottawa, Toronto, Calgary, Vancouver, Montreal, and Halifax. (Try www.housepriceindex.ca/.) And the

Canada Housing and Mortgage Corporation also provides free online subscriptions to its monthly releases, which contain tons of data for both provincial and local markets; go to the statistics and data page at www.cmhc-schl.gc.ca. MLS.ca is also a great resource for looking at homes, and comparing home prices, in different areas. It has a huge database of listings.

Don't be turned off by problems that are easy and inexpensive to fix, like a wall that needs a new coat of paint, a carpet that needs to be shampooed or ripped out, and dingy curtains or rugs. They can make a home less attractive to buyers and result in a better deal for you.

Katie and her husband picked their condo because it was in one of the most desirable urban neighbourhoods in their city, with a low crime rate and a short commute time to downtown offices. It was also within easy walking distance of parks, restaurants, and other attractions. They figured the condo was underpriced because it didn't come with a parking spot, so they checked to be sure. Sure enough, they found that its price was in fact lower than similar listings nearby. But they also knew that there was inexpensive parking very close by. In addition, the building was new, and the condo had two bedrooms and two bathrooms, while much of what they'd seen in their price range only had one bedroom and one bathroom. They realized that not having a parking spot would mean that if they resold the condo, they couldn't charge as much as other units in their building that came with a spot. But the price they paid was low enough that they were confident the value of their condo would increase enough to compensate over time. Indeed, after they bought it in late 2004, their condo increased by $200,000 in value. That's not a typical rate of appreciation—certainly not if you bought now. But it's reasonable to expect that if you buy a home or condo in a desirable neighbourhood that costs less than nearby listings, the value of your home is going to go up over time.

But it's worth discussing with each other whether you'd like to move into a larger place in the next few years, or whether the kinds of homes you can afford now are those you could stay in for several years.

Pick the Right Mortgage for You

There are two main types of mortgages: fixed rate and variable rate. Fixed rate, closed-term mortgages are fixed for a one- to ten-year term. The shorter the time period, generally, the lower the interest rate (they're affected by the price of government bonds and the bond yield). But you're taking a chance that rates could be higher at the end of the fixed-rate period. You may pay a bit more for a five-year, seven-year, or ten-year closed-term mortgage, but you'll also have the comfort of knowing exactly what your payment will be for that period of time and how much of it will go towards the principal. As time goes on, more of the mortgage payment typically goes towards the principal and less of the payment goes to the interest.

The other option is the variable-rate or "floating rate" mortgage. The rate for these mortgages is tied directly to the prime rate, which is set by the Bank of Canada, usually through regularly scheduled announcements. In summer 2009, for example, the rate for a competitive variable mortgage was prime (then at 2.25 percent) plus 0.40 percent—or even less in some cases. Historically, variable-rate mortgages have tended to cost less than fixed-rate mortgages when interest rates are fairly stable. When rates change, your payment amount will still remain the same *but* the amount that is applied towards interest and principal will change. If interest rates drop, more of your mortgage payment is applied to the principal balance, which can help you pay off your mortgage faster. But if rates rise, less of the payment is applied to the principal. And rates can change from month to month.

When you calculate how much you can afford to borrow to buy your home, keep in mind that most mortgage loans have four parts:

1. **The principal:** The repayment of the amount you actually borrowed from the lender.
2. **The interest:** An additional payment to the lender on top of the money you've borrowed.
3. **Homeowners' insurance:** An amount to insure the property against loss from fire, smoke, theft, and other hazards (required by most lenders).

4. **Property taxes:** The annual city/county taxes assessed on your prop-
    erty, divided by the number of mortgage payments you make in a year.

You can discuss various options and go through different calculations with
your mortgage broker or lender. He or she will also help give you an idea of
how much you're qualified to borrow. Then spend some time discussing with
each other how much of a loan you're willing to take on, and which type makes
the most sense for both of you.

Smart Cookie Summary

Discussion Questions:

1. When would you like to start a family and/or buy a home?
2. How much do you think you'll need to save up before you start a
    family? (Take into account how long each of you wants to take off
    from work to stay home with the baby.)
3. What price range do you think you'll be able to afford when buying a
    home? (Use the 32- to 40-percent range, as a guide.)
4. How much money do you estimate you'll be able to save to put to-
    wards the down payment?
5. What features are most important to you in a home and why?

Smart Steps:

1. Using the checklists in this chapter, calculate about how much your
    monthly expenses will grow with a baby.
2. Estimate about how much you think you'll need to save to cover expenses
    for the first year of your baby's life. Don't forget to take into account
    any income loss from time away from work. Also, you may want to
    discuss various child care options, depending on whether you have

relatives nearby, how much nannies charge in your area, and the like-lihood that your baby could get into a subsidized daycare.

3. Figure out how much you will be able to afford for a down payment and monthly mortgage, maintenance and tax payments when you're ready to buy. Then use that to determine a price range for homes you can afford.

4. Scout out different neighbourhoods and homes for sale, and talk to friends to see what they like and don't like about living in their neigh-bourhoods, to help you determine where you want to live and why. Check local prices to see whether home prices are rising or falling in the areas where you look, and to see how the prices of the homes you tour compare to recent sales prices of comparable homes.

5. Each of you make a wish list of everything you want in your new home, and prioritize the items (just in case you can't agree on some or can't find a place that has all the features and amenities you want).

chapter 8

Watch Your Dough Grow

How to Make Sure You Live Happily Ever After

Your paycheques may be your largest source of income, but, fortunately, they don't have to be your only one. You've both worked hard for your money; now let your money work hard for both of you. No matter what your goal—whether it's the two-week tropical vacation you want to take, the three-bedroom home you hope to buy, or the long retirement you'd like to spend together at that cottage on the lake—there's a type of investment out there that will help you get it.

In this chapter, we'll walk you through some basic investment options, from simple selections like savings accounts and GICs (guaranteed investment certificates) to more sophisticated strategies. We'll also share some steps you can take as a couple that could help trim your tax bill and boost your returns even more.

Investing is an essential part of the Smart Cookie strategy for making more dough. But we do recognize that with all its acronyms and abbreviations, it's an area of personal finance that can seem complicated, confusing, and even boring at times. So we've tried to stick to plain English and focus on specific investments and strategies that have worked for us and for the couples we've interviewed for this book. This is a meaty chapter, so we've broken it into various sections to make it easier to digest all the information. In the first, we'll focus on figuring out how much you should invest. Then we'll run through some of the accounts you can use to invest. Finally, we'll help you decide how to invest the money in those accounts to reach your short-term, mid-term, and long-term goals. Throughout the chapter, we'll look at specific strategies you can take as a couple to increase your returns.

So, How Much Should You Invest?

As you're deciding how much money you want to invest, and where, we recommend following these simple steps. First, make sure that you are both making regular contributions into your Registered Retirement Savings Plans (or RRSPs). Ideally, you want to strive towards maxing out your annual contributions, but at the very least make sure that you each contribute enough to take advantage of any match your employers may offer. Then, figure out how much you need to set aside to pay off any remaining debts as quickly as possible. You want to make sure that you get rid of any high-interest balances, those on which you're paying interest of 10 percent or more, before you start putting a lot of money into investments outside of your RRSPs. Why? Because you're unlikely to earn as much through your investments as you're paying in interest on your debts. (If you are carrying a balance with a low interest though—say, 2 to 3 percent—you may be better off putting some money into investments while paying it down since you should be able to earn at least 2 or 3 percent, or more, on your investments.)

Once you've gotten rid of the "bad" debt, at least, start putting extra money aside in a high-yield savings or money market account, which you can tap into if you get hit with a big unexpected expense. It's a good idea to aim for having the equivalent of about six months' worth of expenses set aside. If you fear you may need to dip into your savings in the near future—if one of you is worried about getting laid off, for example—you might want to start putting more money aside in savings even as you're paying down your debts. Just be sure that you make paying off any high-interest debt balances a priority.

You should also consider opening tax-free savings accounts (TFSAs), which first became available in 2009, either together or in each of your names.

We get into more detail later in the chapter on these accounts, but we love these because they offer two big benefits: First, the accounts can function as your back-up emergency fund, since you can generally withdraw any amount at any time without paying taxes or penalties (though you may be charged a fee by your account provider). The TFSA can also help you save money faster to reach your big-ticket goals, whether it's paying for a wedding or buying a home, since you can use the money in the account to invest in everything from savings deposits to GICs to mutual funds and you don't have to pay taxes on the income you make!

If you have children, emergency savings in place, and you're maxing out your TFSA and RRSP, you may also want to consider an RESP, a registered education savings plan geared towards post-secondary tuition, which we described in Chapter Seven. Or you might want to open one or more non-registered investment accounts. There are no real restrictions on how you invest the money when it comes to them, but you'll have to pay taxes on any income you make (e.g., interest earned) and on any capital gains you realize when you sell investments. We'll give you more information on non-registered investment accounts later in the chapter.

Doug and Megan, the couple in Calgary who are in their 30s, both have RRSPs, totalling more than $80,000 between personal contributions and payroll deductions. They want to start maxing out their annual contributions so that they can both retire by the time they're in their 50s—one of their major goals. They each opened TFSAs last year, to which they're contributing about $500 combined per month, though they plan to increase their contributions in the coming years, with the intent that these accounts are being used in part to help them save enough money for their short-term goal of starting a family. They've also got nearly $6,000 in a savings account, which serves as an emergency fund and can be tapped to cover any unexpected expenses. And Doug has close to $17,000 in a non-registered online brokerage account, much of which he deposited after the stock market appeared to bottom out, so he can take advantage of undervalued stocks. Since they don't need the money in this account any time soon, Doug can hold on to these investments for a while, which should increase the chances that the stocks he buys will increase a lot in value before he and Megan sell them.

Before you put together your month-to-month spending, think first about putting aside a set amount to use towards paying off past debts and investing for your future goals. Yes, you also have to pay your bills and expenses. But you want to reserve a minimum amount each month to put towards your debt and into savings and investments first *then* start divvying up the remaining funds for your everyday expenses and occasional indulgences. Back in Chapter Five, you plugged a number into your spending plan for debt payments, savings, and investments. Do you still think it's enough? If so, start there. You can always make adjustments as you pay off any remaining balances you owe and increase the amounts in your savings and retirement accounts.

A great way to make sure you aren't tempted to trim the amount you've agreed on saving and investing is to arrange with your bank to have money automatically withdrawn at the beginning of each month from your personal or joint chequing accounts and deposited into your TFSA, savings, or retirement accounts. This way, you'll both get used to having that money taken out and adjust your spending accordingly, instead of spending your money and then putting whatever's left into your debt payments, savings, and investments. Basically, you're paying yourselves first so that you can be sure that you're on track to reach your goals. Of course, you can always increase the amount that you have automatically transferred as you pay off debts and bulk up your savings, or add more yourselves later in the month.

Once you've both decided on an amount you can start setting aside each month for debt payments, savings, and investments, you need to figure out how much you're going to put towards each one. Remember in Chapter Four when we asked you to prioritize some of the big-ticket items from your perfect day and estimate about how much you'll need to get them? Let's take a closer look at that list. What's the time frame for each goal? And what smaller goals would you like to accomplish in the meantime? Maybe you both want to take a spring vacation somewhere. Or you want to buy a computer or a new couch. Whatever your short-term goals, write them down in your notebook, too, along with an estimate of how much each will cost. Then discuss them together. You should be able to identify some short-term goals, which you want to reach in the next year or two; some mid-term goals, which you'd like to achieve in the next three to ten years; and some long-term goals, for which you've got a decade or more to save. This list will help you both determine what strategy will be the most effective in helping you reach all of your goals.

As you try to figure out how you want to allocate your money, ask yourselves

- How much debt do we owe? How quickly do we want to pay it off?
- How much money will we need to put towards our balances to have them paid off by our target date?
- Are we paying more in interest than we could be earning from other investments? (If you're paying interest that's more than 5 percent, you're still probably better off putting extra funds towards that balance. You'd make a lot less than that if you had a high-yield savings account in 2009, and there's no guarantee that you'd make more than 5 percent on stocks, bonds, or GICs in the period in which you'd still be paying off your debt. On the other hand, if you've gotten the interest rate down to 2 or 3 percent on your debt, you could invest some of that money in five-year GICs, which were yielding 2.5 percent or more in mid-2009, and conceivably come out ahead. Bankrate.ca is a good source for comparing rates on savings accounts and GICs.)
- Are we each contributing at least as much to our RRSPs as our employer has offered to match?
- What's the maximum we could contribute to our RRSPs annually? How close are we to reaching that amount? When do we need to start maxing out our contributions to feel confident that we'll have enough for retirement?
- How much savings do we have combined? Is it enough to cover six months' worth of expenses? If not, how much more do we need to save to reach that amount?

- How much would we like to put into a high-yield savings or money market account each month and how much would we like to put into tax-free savings accounts? (If you're close to having six months' worth of expenses covered in your bank accounts, you might direct more into your TFSAs.)
- How much would we each like to contribute to our RRSPs versus our TFSAs? (Keep in mind that contributions to RRSPs may be deducted from your income when you pay taxes, up to a certain limits, which we get into below, while contributions to TFSAs are made with after-tax dollars, though eventual withdrawals are tax free. How much you want to contribute to each depends a lot on your goals.)

Take some time and think about how much you really want to set aside to reach your goals. It can be a different amount each month, particularly as you pay off any obligations. You can start with one low amount that you know you can easily put aside for investing next month and then adjust as you go along. Don't be discouraged if you can't afford to invest a lot of money right now. As you'll see in a moment, a little investment can add up to a lot of savings thanks to the magic of compounding.

Three Cheers for Compounding

Remember back in Chapter Six when we explained how card issuers add interest to your credit card balance each day, so that you are actually being charged interest on your interest? This is why, if you had an 18-percent annual percentage rate and a $100 starting balance but only paid the interest off each month, you'd still pay more than $18 in interest over the course of the year. It might seem like nothing, but it can really add up. If you had a credit card balance of just $500 and paid the interest *plus* 1 percent of your balance each month, it would still take you more than *seven* years to pay off your balance and you'd end up paying another $370 in interest—almost as much as you'd borrowed! When you owe money, compounding—basically interest charged on your interest—works against you. But the opposite is true when you're investing.

When the gains you make on your investment begin to earn money, too, and *those* returns start to earn money, and so on, your results increase exponentially. Even if you only contributed $100 a month, and earned a return of about 8 percent, your investment would balloon to nearly $35,000 in 15 years!

Sure, it takes time for compounding to really work its magic, and if you invest in stocks there's always the risk that they will decrease in value, too—as many of us have learned in the last year and a half. (That's why diversification is so important, but we'll get to that later in this chapter.) It truly is amazing, though, how much your money can grow through compound interest, even with very little effort and no additional deposits.

If you've put off investing because you think you need to have a lot of money in order to earn a lot, we hope we've proven here that you don't. Claire, the Toronto teacher with the newborn, had to cut her RRSP contributions after they had their baby. But she continued to put $100 into her account each month in part because she knows that even $1,200 a year will add up. In fact, even if you can only spare $25 a month, your first year's investment ($300) can earn you thousands of dollars over the long run.

We'll go through some of the various investment options in more detail later in this chapter. But first let's go through the different types of accounts you can use for investing.

Registered Retirement Savings Plans (RRSPs): This is a tax-deferred fund, meaning you won't pay taxes until you withdraw your money in retirement. One big benefit with your RRSP contributions is that you can deduct them from your total annual income when you are calculating your income tax for that year. These are an especially great idea if you don't have a pension plan or a group retirement fund through your job.

Don't have one yet? Setting up your RRSP account can be as easy as downloading the application forms, signing them, and putting them into an envelope with a cheque to start your account. You can use an online broker or open an account at your bank. You've got a couple options when you set one up.

A "managed RRSP" is a government-registered bank account that holds investments and is looked after by your financial institution. With a managed RRSP you may be restricted to GICs (Guaranteed Investment Certificates), Canada Savings Bonds, and a limited selection of mutual funds. The expenses can vary widely, depending on the types of investments held in your account and the way in which they're managed. (Generally speaking, the more under management and the more activity, the higher the fees.)There may also be a minimum initial investment. Your advisor should be able to give you more information on minimum requirements and fees associated with your account.

If you select a self-directed RRSP instead, you're choosing to manage your retirement assets yourself. You'll have many investment decisions to make, but with these decisions comes more control. If you use an online brokerage to set up your self-directed account, it will be nearly identical to any other online investment account you might have. Commissions are charged on each trade and most online brokerages also require a minimum initial investment, usually between $500 and $2,000. Each time you buy or sell an investment, the online brokerage also typically charges a fee or commission. One big benefit to this type of RRSP is that you can hold GICs and Canada Savings Bonds, stocks, bonds, and a much wider variety of mutual funds from third-party companies than you could with a managed RRSP. (We'll go into each of these in more details later in the chapter.)

Keep in mind that there's a limit to the amount you can contribute to any RRSP each year. It's often the equivalent of about 18 percent of your earned income for the previous year, as long as that's less than the maximum contribution allowed. For 2010, that maximum contribution limit is $22,000. Also, be aware that the Canadian Revenue Agency generally won't let you withdraw your money until you're 59-and-a-half years old without paying a 10-percent penalty in addition to taxes. There are two exceptions, though, that you should keep in mind:

smart S€ bite

SHOULD YOU GET A SPOUSAL RRSP? If you're married and one of you has a much higher income than the other, or a lot more saved for retirement, you might consider opening a spousal RRSP, too. These are just like regular RRSPs but with one key exception: Contributions are made by the higher-income spouse into the lower-income spouse's plan. (If the one with the lower income already has an RRSP, you'll need to set up a separate plan to accept spousal contributions.) What's the advantage of setting up a spousal RRSP? You can reduce your combined taxes on your current income *and* on the retirement income you'll get later. By contributing to the other's RRSP on behalf of the spouse who has lower (or no) earnings, the higher earner can claim the tax deduction, reducing your total taxes for the year. (If you're earning more you're typically in a higher tax bracket, so you can get a larger tax break than your spouse would.)

You'll both benefit from this set-up when you retire, too. Since the RRSP is in the lower-earning spouse's name, you'll each have approximately the same income in retirement, so you reduce your overall income tax. In other words, some of the higher earner's income has been shifted to the other spouse, who will pay tax on that income at a lower marginal rate. Keep in mind that you cannot exceed your RRSP contribution limit, though, within your limits, you can contribute to your own plan, a spousal plan, or some combination of the two. Also, be aware that the lower-income spouse must wait three years after the last contribution was made to the spousal plan before withdrawing the money.

- **The Home Buyer's Plan (or HBP)**, which we discussed in the last chapter, allows you to borrow money from your RRSPs without having to pay a withholding tax or penalty. The maximum amount that each of you can borrow from your RRSP is limited to $25,000 (so, between you, you could borrow up to $50,000, as of 2009). You'll each have a 15-year period to pay back the money you borrowed from your RRSPs. After that time, however, the opportunity to replace the borrowed money is permanently lost.

- **The Lifelong Learning Plan (or LLP)** allows either of you to borrow money to go to school (though you cannot use the RRSP funds to finance your kids' education). The maximum amount that you can withdraw from one RRSP is $20,000, but there is an *annual* limit of $10,000. There's no restriction on the number of times you can participate in the plan over your lifetime though. So in the year after you repay the funds you borrowed, you can participate in the LLP again and withdraw up to $20,000 over a new qualifying period. Repaying an RRSP withdrawal from the Lifelong Learning Plan doesn't have to start until five years after the first withdrawal. Once your repayments begin, you will have ten years to pay the money back to your RRSP before the opportunity to replace these funds is gone.

Tax-Free Savings Accounts (TFSAs): This new type of account, which was created in 2009, is similar to an RRSP in that it helps you save for long-term goals and provides tax benefits, but there are some notable differences. The contributions you make to the TFSA are made with after-tax dollars, so you cannot deduct them from your tax bill. But you don't have to pay taxes on the withdrawals you make—not even on any capital gains or income you've earned! And you can withdraw funds from your TFSAs any time for any reason without penalty. The amount you withdraw can be replaced at any time in the future, without reducing that year's contribution limit. The annual contribution limit for 2009 was $5,000 per person, but it's indexed to inflation, so it should be higher this year and in the future. You can also make contributions to your spouse's or common-law partner's TFSA on behalf of him or her, up to that person's contribution limit. (So you can actually contribute more than $5,000 yourself, as long as anything over $5,000 is in your partner's name and account.) Another benefit: If you aren't able to contribute the full $5,000 limit, you can carry forward any unused contribution room into the future. Though you can use the money from this account for short-term or mid-term goals, try to re-place the funds you borrow promptly. Remember that the longer you can take advantage of the tax-free growth, the greater the benefit.

Doug and Megan both opened TFSAs after they became available in 2009, but neither of them expected to max out their contributions last year. (They were still putting the bulk of their money into their RRSPs.) So they were glad to know that they could carry over any amount below the limit that they didn't put in the year before. They both plan to put more into their TFSAs this year, and take advantage of some of the carry-over room they've got.

Like the RRSPs, TFSAs can be managed or set up as a self-directed (or multiple investment/multiple supplier) account. If you choose a managed (or single supplier) TFSA, as Doug and Megan did, you can select between single investment or multiple investment options. With a single investment TFSA you must pick just one type of investment, like a savings account or a GIC. The advantage is that they're simple to use and usually come with no fees. The downside is that you're limiting yourself to one type of investment, and if you want to transfer from one type of investment to another down the road, it can be burdensome. Multiple investment TFSAs offer many different types of investments within the TFSA, though all from the financial institution's own group of investments. They can be a combination of savings accounts, GICs, or mutual funds. The advantage of these types of TFSAs is that you can keep better track of all your investments within one TFSA and you can transfer from one type of investment to another within your account with-out much hassle.

With a self-directed TFSA, you decide how the money is invested. And you typically have a wide range of options—from Canada Savings Bonds to corporate bonds, stocks, and mutual funds. Many of these types of funds charge a $100 to $200 annual fee, and some may also charge activity or termination fees. So ask about any fees related to the account before you open it.

If you don't think you have enough to contribute to RRSPs and TFSAs, or aren't sure how much to contribute to each since you don't have enough to contribute the maximum to both, consider this: If you're in a higher tax bracket now than you think you will be in retirement, you might want to put the bulk of your contributions into your RRSPs (since you can deduct your contributions from your income now, cutting your tax bill, and when you pay taxes on the withdrawals you should be in a lower tax bracket so you won't owe so much). If you're in a low tax bracket now and expect that you'll be in a higher one in the future, and in retirement, you might focus on maxing out your TFSAs now. Why? Because the tax deductions you'd get from RRSP contributions now may not have much of an impact on your tax bill, but you could really benefit from not having to pay taxes on the TFSA withdrawals later. If you expect your incomes to be about the same now and in retirement, then divide your contributions between the two, since you'll get benefits from each.

Non-Registered Investment Accounts: If you're maxing out your annual contributions to your RRSPs and TFSAs, and have an interest in doing additional investing, you may also want to open one or more non-registered investment accounts. These accounts typically offer many investment options, but you'll have to pay tax on any income you make (e.g., interest earned) and on any capital gains you realize when you sell investments.

The most common type—and the one we recommend—is a cash account, in which you deposit a specific amount of money that you can then manage as you want. You can use it, for example, to buy GICs, mutual funds, money market funds, and Canadian or foreign stocks and bonds. In the meantime, the money left in the account is earning a little interest.

You can always go to a brokerage office to set up an investment account in person, but you certainly don't have to do so. There are numerous online brokerages—as well as online services offered by traditional brick-and-mortar institutions—that allow you to put money into an account and then buy or sell stocks or other products online (for a fee, of course). These range from no-frills discount brokers like E*Trade Canada and Qtrade Investor to more service-oriented discount brokers like TD Waterhouse or RBC Direct Investing to a full-service brokerage like RBC Dominion Securities or BMO Nesbitt Burns.

As you're deciding where to open an online account, consider what level of service you require and how much money you have to invest. You might start by buying mutual funds through a discount broker, for example, and then as you accumulate more wealth and have other needs, move to a full-service brokerage, which offers a wider and more sophisticated selection of investment products but for a higher price tag. Here are five factors to consider when you begin your search:

1. **Trade Commissions and Fees**. This is how much it will cost you to buy stocks or other products through the account. Check to see if your online broker offers flat-fee commissions, so regardless of how many shares you buy or the stock price or type of order, you'll pay exactly the same amount every time you trade. (With some brokerage firms, the fee you pay will change based on the type or size of the order you place.) Also, be sure to ask about other fees, like inactivity fees, in which you're charged if you don't place enough trades in a certain period of time.

2. **Customer Service**. There are minimum levels of customer service that all brokers should provide. For example, you should be able to contact someone if you have technical or other problems, and get help in a reasonable amount of time. But when you're deciding how much more service you want, think about how often you or your partner may want to speak to someone and how much advice you need. If you're considering a full-service brokerage, look closely at the range of customer services the firms provide and how much each will cost you. With a discount brokerage, you're largely on your own, though you often have access to research tools. If you or your partner is pretty knowledgeable about investing, and feels comfortable with

the amount of research available online, you may not need a full-service firm. Katie and Nick, for example, prefer using a discount brokerage in part because they really enjoy doing their own research, using the brokerage site's tools.

3. **Trading Tools.** Trading successfully is a lot easier when you have the tools and resources to research the stocks, bonds, or funds you want to buy and to execute your trades quickly and conveniently, or when you have a professional advisor providing you with recommendations on what to buy (as at a full-service brokerage). With discount brokerages, you are largely doing the work on your own, but even a low-cost brokerage should be giving you access to a wide variety of tools to help you make the most of each trade. These can range from access to real-time stock prices and live finance news feeds to sophisticated financial planning tools, fundamental and technical data on stocks and bonds, and market research reports. Ask your broker what tools you'll be able to use for free, based on the account you choose to open.

4. **Account Minimums.** You may think you signed up for $4.95 trades with a discount broker, for example, until you place that first order and get charged $15.95 because you didn't deposit enough money into your account. Check to see if the price you pay per transaction is the same regardless of how much you have in your account. Some brokers have different tiered accounts, so that you may pay more per transaction if you have less in your account (or don't agree to make a certain number of trades per year). Keep in mind that the minimum account requirements for full-service brokers, who often specialize in high net worth clients, are generally higher than for discount brokers. So if you don't have much to invest, your account may not get as much attention from a top-tier, full-service broker as his (or her) larger accounts do.

5. **Investment Options.** Both discount and full-service brokerages provide a range of investment products from which to choose, including stocks, bonds, GICs, or mutual funds. Many also offer other options,

such as chequing accounts and credit or debit cards. Be aware that some brokers may charge more to invest in particular products, so be sure to check what the fee is for each type of purchase. You may also earn interest on the money that you have not yet invested (the money that is still sitting in your account), which is a nice bonus. It's often not much, but you should ask about the yields on the various "core" accounts that may be available, from which you can draw money to purchase other types of investments.

There are more than a dozen online brokerage firms in Canada. If you and your partner are looking for guidance in choosing one, the *Globe and Mail* (www.theglobeandmail.com) offers an annual ranking of online brokers based on criteria like costs and fees; customer satisfaction; tools and research available; website utility (how easily you can get the information you need from the site, for example); website security; and the quality of the trading (how easy is it to trade and how quickly the trades go through, for example). Qtrade Investor has topped the list for two years in a row, besting 13 other contenders in 2009. The independent (meaning non bank–owned) online brokerage scored high in part because of its low commissions and the kind of research it offers to investors. It was followed in the rankings by E*Trade Canada, TD Waterhouse, BMO InvestorLine, and Credential Direct. Two new brokers also made the top ten: Questrade, a small independent firm, and Trade-Freedom, which was acquired by Scotiabank. Rankings like these are helpful, but don't forget to look at all the factors that are important to you. Ultimately, you want to find a brokerage firm that best fits your needs.

In addition to their high-yield savings account, two tax-free savings accounts, and two RRSPs, Katie and Nick chose to open a non-registered investment account with a discount online brokerage that charges them less than $20 a trade. They use the money in the high-yield savings account for short-term goals like vacations or for emergency expenses. Like Doug and Megan, they consider their non-registered investment account an additional way to save for mid- to long-term goals. They only invest a few thousand dollars through the brokerage account, just in case their investments go down (as they did in 2008). But they enjoy doing the research and feel like they're gaining more experience, expertise, and confidence as investors. They also like to be able to bet on young companies that might carry more risk but that might also provide better returns than the more conservative funds they typically invest in through their RRSPs or TFSAs. Even though they are assuming more risk, it's a calculated risk, as they spend a lot of time researching and evaluating the companies before they invest in them.

Of course, stocks aren't the only option when you're investing. Now that we've gone through some of the accounts available, let's go through the options you have for investing the money in those accounts in more detail.

Short-Term Investing

You probably have some short-term goals you're saving money for, whether it's an upcoming vacation, a new piece of furniture, or maybe a class one or both of would like to enroll in next year. Whatever your goal, you're going to want access to your money in a relatively short period: three months, six months, or a year or so. For these time frames, you probably don't want to invest in stocks or bonds. You don't want to risk losing any of the money you saved, and you want to make sure that you can withdraw it when you need it without risk of penalty. You've got three main options from which to choose. We'll go through the benefits of each so you can decide what's best for you:

1. **Savings account.** This is probably the first place you thought about putting that money, and there's nothing wrong with that. It's safe as long as you put your money in a bank that is insured by the Canadian Deposit Insurance Corporation (CDIC), which will reimburse you up to $100,000 if your bank fails or goes bankrupt. (If you've got more than $100,000 in savings, kudos to you! You may want to divide it among accounts at CDIC-insured banks to stay below that maximum in any

one account, as the limit applies to each separate account.) It's easy to set up a savings account and to withdraw money from it, and you can even earn a little interest. Traditionally, savings accounts provide pretty modest returns: generally around 1 percent or less. But you can shop around for high-yield accounts. At times, they've had interest rates as high as 3 percent or more. (The rate fluctuates, so keep an eye on it.)

2. **Money market fund.** This is not a bank account. It is a particular type of mutual fund that invests in a bundle of conservative securities like certificates of deposit (CDs) and federal and provincial treasury bills. This means the money you invest in a money market fund is used for short-term loans to various Canadian companies and government bodies. Money market funds usually pay better interest rates than a conventional savings account, but you're assuming slightly more risk. Money market funds are not covered by CDIC insurance. While investor losses are extremely rare, they are possible.

3. **Guaranteed Investment Certificates (GICs).** These offer you a guaranteed rate of return over a fixed period of time and are most commonly issued by banks or financial institutions. You invest a fixed sum of money—a minimum of at least $500—for a fixed term (anywhere from 30 days to five years or more). If you redeem your GIC before it matures, though, you may have to pay an "early withdrawal" penalty and/or forfeit a portion of the interest you earned. In return for leaving the money alone, the issuing bank or institution pays you interest, typically at regular intervals. When you cash in or redeem your GIC after the time period ends, you get the money you originally invested plus any additional interest you earned. This is a great investment to make when you get a big sum of money (say, a bonus at work) and know that you won't need it for a specific time period. GICs typically provide the best returns of the three options here, and any with a term of five years or less are CDIC-insured up to $100,000 per name and per account, so they carry very little risk. The only downside is that you cannot withdraw your money—at least not without the possibility of

giving up some returns—before the end, or maturation date. Make sure not to agree to an automatic rollover of your investment either. Ask to be contacted within ten days of your GIC maturation date, so you can decide then whether to renew the GIC or withdraw the funds. Your best bet is often to redeem the GIC and then, if you don't need the money, shop around for another high-interest vehicle to invest it in.

Mid- to Long-Term Investing

When you open an RRSP, a TFSA, or a regular brokerage account, you often have a range of mid- to long-term investment options from which to choose. We're going to go through four of them: bonds, stocks, mutual funds, and exchange-traded funds (ETFs).

When some of us did research on these and were describing them to the whole group, we decided to use an analogy we could all relate to: our closets. Think of it this way: If these investments are like clothes, bonds would be the basic, if somewhat boring, essentials that you need to build your wardrobe— a plain white button-down shirt, a pair of straight-leg jeans, and other staples that you can count on wearing for years. Stocks would be the more stylish additions that may seem a bit riskier—maybe they'll be out of fashion next year and seem like a bad investment—but also have a lot of upside potential: the sleeveless, beaded top you splurged on last summer that became your favourite shirt, drawing compliments from your partner and your friends, or the trendy, intentionally ripped jeans you bought your partner. Mutual funds look a lot like your closet should: a mix of basics you can count on and other pieces you're betting will boost the total value of your wardrobe (though there's a risk they may not). So if one item falls out of a fashion or loses its value, you should have plenty of other pieces to offset the loss. Exchange-traded funds are a bit like mutual funds, but they trade like a stock so you can sell them at any time. If the ETF price has gone up, it's like being able to sell all the clothes in your closet to an eager taker who's willing to buy them for more than you paid. Nice. Of course ETFs, like stocks, can also lose their value, meaning you either have to hold on to them longer and hope for a rebound or sell them at a loss. So pick carefully and plan on holding them for a while.

Here are more details on each:

• **Bonds.** This is basically a way for companies and municipal, provincial, and federal governments to raise money from investors. When you "loan" them the money (i.e., buy a bond), you get a record that stipulates how much you paid, a mutually agreed-upon fixed interest rate, how often interest will be paid, and the term of the bond. They're very similar to guaranteed investment certificates, except that they are issued by the government or other corporations and large institutions, and they are not CDIC-insured. Bonds are riskier than GICs but less risky than stocks. Still, it's best to avoid "junk" bonds. Sometimes called "high-yield" bonds—or non-investment grade bonds—these carry a higher risk of default and, therefore, the loss of your investment. If you plan to buy a bond, it's always a good idea to check its rating before you buy it. Ratings are issued and published by three major companies: Moody's, Standard & Poor's, and the Canadian-based Dominion Bond Rating Service.

If you're looking for a particular company or governmental entity, you can search the agencies' websites (moodys.com, standardandpoors. com or dbrs.com). Press releases on rating changes from agencies are also reported on all the major newswires, so it's not hard to find them through your favourite search engine by typing in the name of the company and "bond rating." Look for ratings that are at least considered "investment grade": R1 through R2 (high) for short-term debt and AAA or AA for long-term debt at Dominion; P-1 or P-2 for short-term debt and Aaa through Baa3 for long-term debt for Moody's; A-1 for short-term debt and AAA through BBB for long-term debt for Standard & Poor's. Generally speaking, you want to steer clear of bonds that are rated much lower, which may be considered speculative or junk bonds. Though these bond issuers may try to tempt you with higher returns, the bonds also carry the most risk of defaulting—in other words, not paying you back on time, or at all.

- **Stocks.** In the simplest terms, stocks are a way for you to own parts of businesses. A share of stock represents a proportional share of ownership in a company. As the real or perceived value of the company changes, the value of the share in that company also rises and falls. You make money when the share price increases, as well as from dividends. These are payments taken from a company's earnings and given to shareholders at regular intervals. (Companies aren't required to provide dividends to common shareholders, but many older companies do.) Some companies, of course, are riskier than others. If you invest in a "blue chip" company, a term given to large, well-established, and well-respected companies like Bell Canada, Suncor Energy, or Royal Bank of Canada, your returns may be lower than if you invest in a smaller, newly public company, but your risk is expected to be lower as well. It's not impossible that any of those three companies would declare bankruptcy, but it's unlikely. If you're each under 40, we recommend you invest most of your portfolio in stocks. Although there's more volatility (or ups and downs) with stocks—as we've definitely seen in the last two years—they've historically had higher returns than bonds have. So, if you're not planning to retire for at least ten years, you should have enough time to bounce back from any dips in the stocks' value and benefit from their generally higher rate of return over the long run.

- **Mutual funds.** These are a way for you to pool your funds with other investors to buy large amounts of stocks, bonds, or both. Basically, you are investing in a fund run by a professional that, in turn, buys shares of stock and bonds issued by companies and governments. You can buy a mutual fund directly through a mutual fund company, through any of the major banks in Canada or through a stockbroker or an investment advisor. A mutual fund representative can guide you on your first purchase. But you should also do some research on your own on sites like www.globeinvestor.com and www.morningstar.ca or Yahoo! Finance, where you can find some of the best performers in particular categories, from funds that only invest in health-related stocks to those that invest in a variety of companies that are considered "large-cap" because their overall value, based on their stock price, is $5 billion or more. Then have another conversation to confirm what is best for you. When you invest in a mutual fund, you are buying shares (or units) of the mutual fund, and any growth in its investments is passed on to you, minus fees and expenses. Each fund manager has his or her own investment philosophy so shop around to find one that matches your taste and your threshold for risk. For example, some funds mirror popular indices like the S&P/TSX Composite Index while other fund managers seek out and invest in companies they think are under-valued or have high-growth potential.

Investing in mutual funds has some distinct advantages. The funds often invest in an array of stocks and bonds, so you tend to lower your risks through diversification: While one stock or bond may drop in value, another may do ex-traordinarily well, so you still come out on top. Also, you can typically sell your shares quickly and at a fair price if you need the money. Finally, your invest-ments will be monitored by a professional money manager, who should have more experience and expertise—not to mention time—than you do to oversee the investments. (Though that doesn't mean they're immune to losses either, as we've seen in the recent downturn.)

The downside: Mutual funds are *not* guaranteed or insured by the CDIC. So you can lose money investing in mutual funds. Also, you'll still have to pay charges (like sales or service), fees (upfront or when you cash out), and other expenses, regardless of how the fund performs. If you choose a deferred service option there may be a declining fee to get out. But you can also buy mutual funds on a front-end basis, in which the advisor will charge upfront but you won't have to pay a fee to get out. Some mutual funds cost more because they cost more to run.

• **Exchange-Traded Funds (ETFs).** These are similar to the index mutual funds except that they trade like a stock on the Toronto Stock Exchange. What does that mean? The funds track an index of specific sector stocks (buying only shares in biotech companies, for example, or only in companies that make up the S&P 500), but you can actually buy or sell them like a stock throughout the trading day. If you put in a sell order with a mutual fund, for example, you gen-erally have to wait until the end of the day when the "net asset value" is deter-mined to find out the price you receive. But with an ETF, you can sell whenever you want and the order will go through in real time, so you'll get the current market price. They are easy to buy; you just need a brokerage account (you may also be able to buy them through your TFSA or RRSP). And there's generally no minimum. They can also be more tax efficient than traditional mutual funds because you don't usually pay taxes on them till you sell your shares, hopefully at a profit, and pay taxes on your gains, whereas mutual funds often distribute their capital gains to the investor annually. The downside? It's a passive investment, meaning there's no manager monitoring and choosing the securities in the fund. You have to stay on top of it yourself. And if the underlying index drops significantly, so will the fund.

For the most part, you can make and monitor your basic investments yourself. But as your portfolio grows or becomes more sophisticated, you may want to hire a financial advisor to help. Yes, it will cost you—either a flat fee or a percentage of the money he or she helps you manage. But a good financial planner can be well worth the expense, especially once you've got a family, a mortgage, and a substantial amount of money to manage. Many are qualified to do much more than just tell you how to invest your money. They can counsel you on everything from taxes to insurance to estate planning.

You may need to interview more than one advisor, since you really want to find someone you both trust who understands not just your investment goals, but your life goals as a couple. Make sure to ask about fees and commissions, and request to see any certificates he or she has and find out what the certification entailed. Look for those who are certified financial planners (CFPs). These advisors have been licensed by the Financial Planners Standards Council, a not-for-profit organization that promotes and enforces tough standards for financial planners. (There are approximately 17,000 advisors with the CFP designation in Canada now.) You can look up CFPs and check to see if a planner's licence is in good standing on the council's site at www.fpsccanada.org.

Generally speaking, you'd like a financial advisor or broker who will not only save you the time and energy it takes to stay on top of your investments, but will help you enjoy returns that are better than you would have gotten on your own. So if you don't see good returns on your investments, consider finding someone else or managing the money yourself. It also helps to seek out mentors you admire and whom you can trust as you decide on your investment strategy. They can share advice from their experience and expertise, and you won't have to pay for it.

Though you may prefer to spend more time on it, you may only need a few minutes every week or month to check the progress on your investments and to decide whether to change your allocation, make additional trades, or increase your contributions, after you've made your initial decisions. One of you may want to take the lead if you enjoy investing, but make sure that you're both involved in any decisions you make and that you are both aware of where and how your money is invested at any given time. (The same holds true if you have an advisor.) Don't be discouraged by any short-term losses. You can generally expect the value of your portfolio to increase between 5 and 10 percent annually on average over the long run. Just keep your money diversified in a mix of domestic and foreign stocks and bonds, funds and ETFs, savings accounts and GICs. Take advantage of the extra boost you get from employer matches and from the tax benefits that RRSPs and TFSAs offer. Invest regularly. And make sure that your investment choices reflect both your short-term and your long-term goals. Then you can sit back and relax, knowing that even when you're not working, your money is working for you.

Smart Cookie Summary

Discussion Questions:

1. What are your short-term, mid-term, and long-term financial goals?
2. Do you have enough money in your savings account to cover six months of expenses?
3. Are you taking advantage of both RRSPs and TFSAs?

4. How well do your current investment choices match your goals?

5. What types of investments are most appealing to you now? Why?

Smart Steps:

1. List your short-term, mid-term, and long-term goals in your notebook.

2. Beside each list of goals, write down about how much money you both think you'll need to achieve those goals and when you'd like to reach them.

3. For each list of goals, write down one or two investment options that match your time frame, your tolerance for risk, and the amount of money you need.

4. If you're planning to invest in stocks, bonds, or mutual funds, do some research to determine which funds might provide the best return for your time frame. (Good resources include www.morningstar.com, www.globeinvestor.com, and www.canadianmoneysaver.ca, among others.)

5. For each of the types of accounts that interest you—RRSPs, TFSAs, RESPs, non-registered investment accounts, and savings and money market accounts—research the banks, fund companies, or investment or brokerage firms that offer them, comparing their rates, returns, and other features.

Afterword:

Live Your Richest Life Together

Our last book, *The Smart Cookies' Guide to Making More Dough*, was primarily geared towards women. But after the book came out, we kept hearing from women—and men—who were in relationships and wanted advice on how to get on track *with* their partners. After being approached time after time, the five of us quickly agreed that this was a natural topic for our second book.

As Smart Cookies, we've all experienced the role money can play in a relationship—both good and bad—and the damage that can be done when we don't address the issues that inevitably come up when we're part of a couple. We also know that there's no one-size-fits-all approach to dealing with finances together. But there some basic steps we can all take to improve our finances and our relationships with our partners, whether we're in a serious long-term relationship, a common-law partnership, or a marriage. Going through the exercises in this book with our partners helped us strengthen our relationships. We hope they did the same for you and your partner.

Each of us has noticed changes in the way we approach money in our personal lives and especially in our relationships. Robyn, for example, used to put a vacation on her credit card rather than admit that she needed a little time to save the money to cover it. Now every goal-setting session she and her partner have includes a discussion about how they will save the money together to achieve the goals they set. Angela used to dread talking about money, but she says she actually looks forward to having money conversations with her partner now that she's seen how easy—and essential—it is to act as a team and work together to reach common goals. Before joining the Smart Cookies, Andrea says she never wanted to discuss finances with her partner either, mostly because she was ashamed of the messy state her money was in. She would have balked at the thought of pooling funds or opening a joint account. But now that she's got her own finances in order, she says she's eager to start the conversation because she knows she can hold up her end of any partnership. Sandra and her boyfriend have now made talking about money a daily habit, treating it as they would any other topic that affects their life together. She's convinced that their relationship is stronger, not just because they're honest and open about their finances but because they're clear on both their goals and how they're going to get the money to reach them. Not only can they see their future together, but they're confident they can afford it.

Katie and Nick, our model Smart Cookie couple, are getting ever closer to living their perfect day every day. They've continued to build wealth through their Smart Cookie lifestyle and their "live on one paycheque and bank the other" philosophy. They are getting close to paying off their condo; they saved to pay cash for a month-long trip to Australia (the one they discussed earlier in this book); and they're still setting aside money so they can expand their family in the next few years.

We know how tough it can seem to try and overcome some of the financial issues that come up when you're part of a couple—especially if you're still trying to get your own finances in order. But we also know that with the right tools and the right approach *every* couple can get there. We've tried to provide those for you in this book, so that you're not just improving your finances but your relationship too. Tackling the topic of money early on and speaking openly and honestly with each other about the issues that come up can save you a lot of stress and heartache down the road. But that's just one of the potential benefits of talking about your finances and planning your financial future together.

We know, both from personal experience and from speaking with dozens of couples, that when you synchronize your financial goals and you agree on the part you'll each play in achieving them, you'll reach them much faster than you could have on your own. By working as a team, you're not only improving your finances but you're building a stronger foundation for your relationship and your future together. We hope that you use the experiences and the advice that we have shared in this book to create the best possible life for yourself and your partner.

If you find you need some help or motivation along the way, though, we encourage you to go to our website: smartcookies.com. We've been working hard to make our site a hub for women and for couples who want information they can use in their everyday life and inspiration to help them stay on track with their goals. We have added a blog that provides you with a closer glimpse of our own personal relationships with money and examples of how we have overcome financial challenges with our partners. You can share your stories too, and submit questions, on our open forum. And if you'd like quick Cookie tips on how to save, spend, and invest smarter, check out our daily "Bite Size Cookies." You can also become a fan on our Smart Cookie Facebook page and follow us on Twitter at www.twitter.com/smartcookies. And be sure to check out our weekly column in Globe Life and GlobeInvestor.com.

Since the release of our first book, the Smart Cookies have become regular media fixtures on the subject of personal finance. In addition to our television series airing on the W and Cosmo Network, we also regularly appear on broadcasts like *Canada AM, CBC Newsworld,* and numerous radio stations across the country. One of the most rewarding aspects of touring the country with our regular media and speaking appearances is hearing the incredible success stories of couples who've overcome the obstacles together. As you put the practices from this book in place and work toward creating your dream life together, we hope you too will share your stories and your insights with us and with others like you through our website.

To living your richest life,

The Smart Cookies

Notes

Chapter One

Page 1 "But as the Motown song made famous by the Beatles goes, 'Your loving gives me such a thrill, but your loving don't pay my bill[s]!'" Janie Bradford and Berry Gordy, Jr. "Money (That's What I Want)." Lyrics. Perf. John Lennon. *With the Beatles.* Parlophone, 1963, accessed June 2009, at: www.lyricsdownload.com/ barrett-strong-money-that-s-what-i-want-lyrics.html.

Page 3 "One 15-year study by Ohio State University (published in the *Journal of Sociology* in 2005) found that those who stay married are able to accumulate nearly *double* the wealth of those who remain single." Jay L. Zagorsky, "Marriage and Divorce's Impact on Wealth," *Journal of Sociology,* Vol. 41, No. 4, pp. 406–24 (2005), accessed June 2009, at: jos.sagepub.com/cgi/content/abstract/ 41/4/406.

Page 4 "The U.S. Census . . . found that the average net worth of all households headed by married couples is nearly $102,000, while single men have an average net worth of $23,700 and single women have an average net worth of just $20,217." U.S. Census Bureau. "Net Worth and the Assets of Households: 2002," April 2008, accessed June 2009, at: www.census.gov/prod/2008pubs/p70–115.pdf.

Page 6 "A poll conducted for the Bank of Montreal in 2008 ranked money as *the* most sensitive topic of conversation among Canadians—ahead of religion, politics, and even weight." CBC News. "Money talk taboo for Canadians compared to love, politics, religion: survey," August 6, 2008, accessed June 2009, at: www.cbc.ca/consumer/story/2008/08/06/survey-money.html.

Page 6 "So it shouldn't be a surprise that in the U.K., the Financial Services Authority found nearly three-quarters of couples have a tough time talking about
money . . ." *The Financial Express.* "Couples think money isn't a sexy topic, says
survey," February 10, 2006, accessed June 2009, at: www.financialexpress.com/
news/couples-think-money-isnt-a-sexy-topic-says-survey/101880/.

Page 7 "One study published in the *Journal of Socio-Economics* found spouses disagreed on everything from how much income and wealth they had to how much
debt they carried." *Ohio State University News.* "Husbands, Wives Don't Agree
on their Financial Status, Study Finds," May 27, 2003, accessed June 2009, at:
researchnews.osu.edu/archive/famfinan.htm.

Page 7 "In a 2006 *Money* magazine survey of 1,000 spouses, about a quarter of the
men surveyed said they thought their wives believed that having the right investments was very important." *Money.* "Men & Women Still Can't Make Cents
of Each Other," March 16, 2006, accessed June 2009, at: www.timeinc.net/fortune/
information/presscenter/money/press_releases/20060319_marriagemoney_
MON.html.

Page 7 "While 70 percent of wealthy wives said they shared the financial decision-
making responsibilities with their spouses in a 2005 survey by PNC Advisors,
fewer than half of their husbands said that was the case." PNC News Releases
archive. "Valentine's Day is a Time for a 'Heart to Heart' About Money Matters,"
2006, accessed June 2009, at: pnc.mediaroom.com/index.php?s=43&item=416.

Chapter Three

Page 53 "You've probably heard of them: Oprah Winfrey has talked about them on
her show." *The Oprah Winfrey Show.* "Go Beyond *The Secret,*" February
2008, accessed June 2009, at: www.oprah.com/slideshow/oprahshow/
slideshow1_ss_ss_20080206/8.

Chapter Four

Page 84 "In a study published in the *Journal of Financial Planning,* researcher Tahira
Hira, a professor of consumer economics and personal finance at Iowa State
University, found that women are twice as likely as men to shop impulsively . . ."
Tahira K. Hira and Olive Mugenda, "Gender Differences in Financial Perceptions,
Behaviors, and Satisfaction," *Journal of Financial Planning.* Vol. 13, Issue 2
(February 2000).

Page 85 "A study presented to the British Psychological Society meeting in April 2009
found women are particularly susceptible to spending sprees in the ten days before
their periods . . ." BBC News. "Shopping Sprees Linked to Periods," March 30,
2009, accessed June 2009, at: news.bbc.co.uk/2/hi/health/7971578.stm.

Page 86 "In its most recent report, the U.S. Bureau of Labor Statistics found that single men in 2007 spent more than twice as much as single women did on alcoholic beverages . . ." Bureau of Labor Statistics. "Table 44. Consumer units of single females by income before taxes: Average annual expenditures and characteristics, Consumer Expenditure Survey, 2006–2007," June 2007, accessed June 2009, at: ftp.bls.gov/pub/special.requests/ce/crosstabs/y0607/sexbyinc/femalinc.txt.

Chapter Six

Page 123 "Household debt in Canada reached an all-time high of $1.3 trillion in 2008, or more than $90,000 per household—and that number is expected to grow." Certified General Accountants Association of Canada. "Where Has the Money Gone: The State of the Canadian Household Debt in a Stumbling Economy," p. 132, March 2009, accessed June 2009, at: www.cga-canada.org/en-ca/ResearchAndAdvocacy/AreasofInterest/DebtandConsumption/Pages/ca_debt_index.aspx.

Page 129 "The foreclosure rate in Canada hasn't been as bad as in the United States, where one in every 398 homes had received a foreclosure filing by May of 2009 . . ." RealtyTrac. "U.S. Foreclosure Activity Decreases 6 Percent in May," June 11, 2009, accessed June 2009, at: www.realtytrac.com/ContentManagement/PressRelease.aspx?channelid=9&ItemID=6655.

Page 131 "There are now more than 68 million credit cards circulating in the country, a jump of more than four million from just a couple of years ago . . ." Rita Trichur and Dana Flavelle. "Fight to cap credit card interest rates, fees heats up," *The Star*, January 24, 2009, accessed June 2009, at: www.thestar.com/Business/article/576545.

Page 131 "By last spring, bank credit card receivables (meaning balances owed) had jumped nearly 9 percent from the year before to $51.5 billion, according to the Bank of Canada." CBC News. "Canadian Households $1.3 trillion in debt," May 26, 2009, accessed June 2009, at: www.cbc.ca/consumer/story/2009/05/26/canada-household-debt854.html.

Page 131 "Personal lines of credit reached a record high of $181 billion outstanding last spring, up more than 20 percent from the year before. And personal bank loans were up more than 8 percent from the year before at $48.5 billion." Ibid.

Page 134 "In May 2009, U.S. President Barack Obama signed the U.S. Credit Card Accountability Responsibility and Disclosure Act, which imposes several new regulations on credit card companies in the United States." Jonathan Chevreau. "New Credit Card Regulations Too Little Too Late?" *Financial Post*, May 22, 2009, accessed June 2009, at: network.nationalpost.com/np/blogs/ wealthy-boomer/archive/2009/05/22/new-credit-card-regulations-too-little-too-late.aspx.

Page 135 "Finance Minister Jim Flaherty also announced some new credit card regulations in May 2009 that are aimed at protecting Canadian consumers.": Eric Lam. "Ottawa Introduces New Credit Card Regulations," *Financial Post*, May 21, 2009, accessed June 2009, at: www.financialpost.com/story.html?id=1615992.

Page 145 "According to the Financial Consumer Agency of Canada, if the financial institution agrees that an error was made . . ." Financial Consumer Agency of Canada. "Understanding Your Credit Report and Score," March 25, 2009, accessed June 2009, at: www.fcac-acfc.gc.ca/eng/publications/CreditReportScore/CCreditReportScore_e.asp#errors.

Page 146 "In the summer of 2009, banks were offering rates of 3 percent or more on three- to five-year GICs." *Canoe Money.* "GIC Rates, " July 1, 2009, accessed June 2009, at: money.canoe.ca/rates/gics.html.

Chapter Seven

Page 150 "According to the most recent report by Manitoba Agriculture, you can expect to spend more than $166,000 to raise a child from birth to age 18." Joan Butcher. "Family Finance: The Cost of Raising a Child: 2004," Manitoba Agriculture, Home Economics Section, July 2004, accessed June 2009, at: web.archive.org/web/20050228043441/http://www.gov.mb.ca/agriculture/homeec/coc2004/cba28s01.html.

Page 151 "An informal 2009 survey of parents by the CBC found that the average daycare costs ranged from $600 to $1,300 *a month* per child in Toronto . . ." CBC News. "Daycare: The Debate over Space," February 11, 2009, accessed June 2009, at: www.cbc.ca/consumer/story/2009/02/06/f-daycare.html.

Page 156 "But tuition costs have been rising about 4.4 percent per year over the last decade. In the 2008–2009 school year, full-time students in undergraduate programs paid on average more than $4,700 per annum, while graduate students paid close to $5,800." Statistics Canada. "University Tuition Fees," October 9, 2008, accessed July 1, 2009, at: www.statcan.gc.ca/daily-quotidien/081009/ dq081009a-eng.htm.

Page 160 "Generally speaking, those monthly housing costs—including mortgage principal and interest, taxes, and heating expenses—shouldn't be more than 32 percent of your gross household monthly income . . ." Canada Mortgage and Housing Corporation. "Are You Financially Ready?" accessed July 1, 2009, at: www.cmhc-schl.gc.ca/en/co/buho/hostst/hostst_002.cfm.

Page 161 "Don't forget to factor in the other upfront costs of buying a home like . . ." Canada Mortgage and Housing Corporation. "How Much Will It Really Cost?" accessed July 1, 2009, at: www.cmhc-schl.gc.ca/en/co/buho/hostst/hostst_003.cfm.

Page 163 "If you're buying your first home, you may also be exempt from paying a property transfer tax (PTT), which can potentially cost in the thousands."

British Columbia Ministry of Finance. "Property Transfer Tax and the First Time Home Buyers' Program," February 2008, accessed July 2009, at: www.sbr.gov.bc.ca/documents_library/brochures/FirstTimeHomeBuyer.pdf.

Page 165 "The Royal LePage Survey of Canadian House Prices, which includes information on seven types of housing in more than 250 neighbourhoods, found prices in most provinces fell . . ." Royal LePage. "Canadian Real Estate Relatively Resilient During First Quarter," April 8, 2009, accessed July 2009, at: www.royallepage.ca/CMSTemplates/AboutUs/Company/CompanyTemplate.aspx?id=1946.

Page 165 "But in May, the Canadian Real Estate Association reported that the average price of existing homes sold nationwide had actually increased, though by less than half a percent." The Canadian Real Estate Association. "MLS Statistics," June 2009, accessed in June 2009, at: www.crea.ca/public/news_stats/statistics.htm.

Page 171 "Last summer, for example, the rate for a competitive variable mortgage was prime (then at 2.25 percent) plus 0.40 percent—or even less in some cases." CanEquity. "Mortgage Rate History," June 24, 2009, accessed June 2009, at: www.canequity.com/mortgage_rate_history.stm.

Chapter Eight

Page 183 "What's the advantage of setting up a spousal RRSP? You can reduce your combined taxes on your current income *and* on the retirement income you'll get later." Peter Diekmeyer. "The Advantages of Spousal RRSPs," Bankrate.com, January 24, 2005, accessed July 2009, at: www.bankrate.com/brm/news/rrsp-rrif/RRSPguide2005Can/spousal-RRSP1.asp.

Page 189 "The *Globe and Mail* (www.theglobeandmail.com) offers an annual ranking of online brokers based on criteria like . . ." Rob Carrick. "Online Broker Survey: Qtrade Wins Again," April 3, 2009, accessed July 2009, at: www.theglobeandmail.com/report-on-business/online-broker-survey-qtrade-wins-again/article786863/.

Resources

Chapter Three

For help with perfect-day exercise estimates for . . .

- A Baby: Several sites offer checklists of what you'll need for a baby, including: www.surebaby.com/baby_checklist.php, www.expectantmothersguide.com, www.canadababyresources.com, www.babyontheway.ca, and www.babycenter.ca. You can estimate prices by checking retailers with online sites like The Bay, Wal-Mart, and Babies "R" Us.
- A Car: Check sites that offer information on car values, include the Canadian Black Book (www.canadianblackbook.com) and CanadianDriver (www.canadiandriver.com), which also has a helpful lease versus loan calculator.
- A Home: Check with a local real estate agent or check home prices at www.mls.ca or www.craigslist.org.

Test drive your dream job:

- You can book a trip and spend a day or more working in your dream job through vocationvacations.com.

Find out what you're worth:

- Payscale.com offers a free salary-comparison report for your job in your city, based on your experience and education, using information from other anonymous users.
- You can also get salary information for jobs by logging on to sites like workopolis.ca or monster.ca.

Chapter Four
Find additional resources and worksheets for adding up your numbers at: www.smartcookies.com.

Chapter Five
Need more information on some of those tips we offered to cut back a little without lowering your standard of living?
- Exercise with friends: Get more information on YMCA rates and locations at: www.ymca.ca.
- Wrinkle creams: Learn more about *Consumer Reports'* study of wrinkle creams at: www.consumerreports.org.
- Internet phone service (or VoIP): Go to www.NextAdvisor.com for a comparison of different VoIP services.
- Be energy-efficient: For more tips on saving energy at home and at work, go to: www.energysavers.gov/.
- Go paperless! Take your pick of online newspapers at www.news.google.ca.
- Swap houses for an inexpensive getaway: www.HomeExchange.com, www.homeforswap.com, www.homeforexchange.com, or www.digsville.com.
- Start your discount travel research here: www.orbitz.com, www.kayak.com, www.hotwire.com, www.travelocity.com, www.sidestep.com, www.bing.com/travel.

Earn extra cash:
- Use craigslist.org to rent your parking space or sell old clothes or other items.
- Rent your home for use as a location for commercials, TV shows, or movies. You can register your home directly with film studios, production companies, and advertising firms, which maintain lists of properties available for shooting. Check out eHow.com for tips, or *Opening Your Door to Hollywood*, a 2006 book by producer James Perry
- Be an extra: You don't need a Screen Actors Guild (SAG) membership or even any acting experience to qualify—just the patience to sit on a set for hours and the flexibility to try out a lot of different costumes and lines. Pay can range from $100 to more than $1,000 a day. Check the classifieds in your local weekly entertainment paper.
- Be a secret shopper: Check out sites like www.sensusshop.com.

For more information on Tax-Free Savings Accounts (TFSAs), go to: www.tfsa.gc.ca or www.taxfreesavingscanada.ca/fees.main.html.

Chapter Six

Student loans:

- For more information on need-based grant programs administered by various Canadian provinces, go to: www.mcgill.ca/studentaid/government/directory.
- To learn more about a wide selection of scholarships from the Association of Universities and Colleges in Canada, including scholarships for mature students, go to Scholarships Canada at: www.scholarshipscanada.com.

Business loans and resources:

- A good resource for general information is Canada Business Services for Entrepreneurs, at: www.canadianbusiness.ca.
- For funding information, check out Industry Canada, at: www.ic.gc.ca.
- For more information on women's groups, visit the website for Women Entrepreneurs in Canada, at: www.wec.ca, the Forum for Women Entrepreneurs, at: www.fwe.org, and Count Me In for Women's Economic Independence, at: www.makemeamillion.org.

Buying a car:

- For ratings and research on the specific models and the best resale values, check the Canadian Black Book online, at: www.canadianblackbook.com.
- For the best deal, try buying directly from the car owner, through classified ads, or through www.craigslist.org.

Trimming transportation costs:

- For more information on the car-sharing service called Zipcar, go to: zipcar.com. (In Toronto also try Autoshare, at: www.autoshare.com.)

Credit card calculator:

- Want to see how long it will take you to pay off your credit card balance— and how much interest you'll pay—if you make just the minimum payment each month? Go to: www.bankrate.com or www.fool.com.

Consumer credit counselling:

- Try calling your creditors directly first.
- If that doesn't work, look for accredited, licensed organizations with certified credit counsellors on the Credit Counselling Canada website, at: www. creditcounsellingcanada.ca, or the Better Business Bureau, at: www.bbb.org.

Getting your credit report and credit score:
- Order your free credit report directly from a credit reporting agency, at: www.equifax.ca and www.transunion.ca.
- For information on credit scores and credit reporting, visit the Financial Consumer Agency of Canada website, at: www.fcac-acfc.gc.ca.
- You're entitled to one free copy of your credit report each year from each of the three major credit bureaus, though they're not required to provide your score. Only one website is authorized to fill orders for the free annual credit report: www.annualcreditreport.com.
- Get your scores directly from a major credit bureau: Equifax Canada (www.equifax.ca), or TransUnion (www.transunion.ca).

Chapter Seven
Buying a home:
- The best place to go online for current home prices—and to find undervalued properties—is the Canadian Real Estate Association's Multiple Listing Service, at: www.mls.ca.
- If you are interested in buying directly from the buyer, check out your local classifieds and www.craigslist.org.
- Looking for the perfect Realtor®? Find your perfect match at: www.howrealtorshelp.ca.
- For more information on the Home Buyers' Plan (HBP) visit the Canada Revenue agency, at: www.cra-arc.gc.ca.
- Compare mortgage rates and calculate mortgage payments at www.bankrate.ca.
- To find out more on monthly housing costs—and to see if you are financially ready to own—check out the Canadian Mortgage and Housing Corporation, at: www.cmhc-schl.gc.ca.

Starting a family:
- Child Care: Your provincial or territorial government may offer subsidized daycare (childcarecanada.org).
- Furnishings: Check out www.ikea.ca for new, inexpensive pieces and Once Upon a Child (www.ouac.com) for gently used finds.
- Diapers: Buy diapers in bulk at wholesale clubs like Costco (www.costco.ca) and sign up at diaper manufacturers' websites to get coupons.
- Car Seats: Visit the Transport Canada site at www.tc.gc.ca for tips on choosing and installing car seats and information on product recalls.
- Baby Benefits: Visit www.servicecanada.gc.ca and www.cra-arc.gc.ca for information on the Universal Childcare Benefit, GST credits, Canada Child Tax Benefit, the Child Disability Benefit, Employee Insurance Maternity Benefits, and child care deductions.

Chapter Eight

Checking out investments:

- A great international resource for all things investment-related is: www.investopedia.com.
- If you are looking for information and ratings on bonds issued by a particular company or governmental agency, search the rating agencies' websites, at: www.moodys.com, www.standardandpoors.com, and Canadian-based Dominion Bond Rating Service, at: www.dbrs.com.
- You can also check out Yahoo! Finance or other personal finance sites to find some of the best fund and individual stock performers in particular categories.
- Try out risk-free investing with an RBC practice account. Visit www.rbcdirectinvesting.com and click on practice accounts.

Mutual funds:

- Thinking about investing in mutual funds? Do your own research, at: www.globeinvestor.com and www.morningstar.ca.

Online investing:

- Some no-frills discount brokers are E*Trade and Qtrade. Check them out, at: www.canada.etrade.com and www.qtrade.ca.
- For service-oriented brokers, try TD Waterhouse and RBC Direct Investing, at: www.tdwaterhouse.ca and www.rbcdirectinvesting.com.
- For full-service brokers in Canada, check out RBC Dominion Securities and BMO Nesbitt Burns, at: www.rbcds.com and www.bmonesbittburns.com.

Retirement:

- Plan wisely with the RRSP Home Buyers' Plan, at: www.car-arc.gc.ca.
- For more information on RRSPs, visit any of the major Canadian banks' websites, and consult www.investopedia.com.
- Looking for someone to help you balance your books? For information on choosing the right certified accountant, check out: www.cica.ca and www.cga-canada.org.

Index

The Smart Cookies are Andrea Baxter, Katie Dunsworth, Robyn Gunn, Sandra Hanna, and Angela Self. Like many women in their twenties and thirties, they were once drowning in consumer debt. Inspired by an episode of the *Oprah Winfrey Show*, the Cookies formed a money group and developed strategies for turning their finances around—without sacrificing their fabulous style or social lives. They are now the authors of the wildly successful book *The Smart Cookies' Guide to Making More Dough*, and run their own company, Smart Cookies Money Mentoring Inc., which is dedicated to helping women improve their financial skills. They tour the country speaking on the topic of personal finance, have a weekly column in the *Globe and Mail*, and appear on local and national television and radio shows. They live in Vancouver and Toronto. www.smartcookies.com

Jennifer Barrett has written about financial issues for the *Wall Street Journal*, the *New York Times*, and *Newsweek*. She lives in New York City with her husband and son.
www.jenniferbarrett.net